THE INSIDER SECRETS:
OF THE WORLD'S MOST SUCCESSFUL MORTGAGE BROKERS

NATE KENNEDY
MARK EVANS

DM Publishing

Deal Maker Publishing, LLC

The Insider Secrets of the World's Most Successful Mortgage Brokers™

© Deal Maker Publishing, LLC

All Rights Reserved. This publication may not be reproduced, stored in a retrieval system, or transmitted in whole or in part, in any form or by any means, electronic, mechanical, photocopying, recording, or otherwise, except for personal use, without prior express written permission of the author.

ISBN #: 978-0-615-17270-5

Printed in the United States of America

This publication is designed to provide competent and reliable information regarding the subject matters covered. However, it is sold with the understanding that the author and publisher are not engaged in rendering legal, financial, or other professional advice. If legal or other expert assistance is required, the services of a professional should be sought. The author and publisher specifically disclaim any liability that is incurred from the use or application of the contents of this book.

Please visit our website at www.DealMakerPublishing.com

The author and publisher would like to acknowledge and thank the participants in this book who have granted us permission to cite their trademarked and copyrighted materials and publications.

Think and Grow Rich® is a registered trademark of The Napoleon Hill Foundation

ACKNOWLEDGMENTS

THIS BOOK IS THE RESULT of the collaboration of many great people and for that, I would like to extend my gratitude and appreciation to:

My parents, for always believing in me and teaching me that I am able to achieve anything I want as long as I stay focused and set my goals high. Thank you so much for everything you have done for me.

My brother and sisters, Nick, Melissa, and Taylor; even though we don't talk or see each other every day you are the best friends that I will always have. I love you all very much.

My nephews and niece, Blake, Brennen, and Jadelyn. You are all full of life and have many great adventures ahead of you. I can't wait to see you all grow up and become great people just like your parents.

My grandparents, for being so loving and caring as I grew up and as I continue into my career. I wish everyone had grandparents like you!

Susan, for being a tremendous support to me in life and my career. You are an amazing person and I am excited for the many great years that we have ahead of us. Who would have thought that one road trip would have created so many opportunities. Thank you and I love you.

Mark Evans DM, who has mentored me through this whole process and has been a true inspiration in my life; I will always remember the day that my life changed on Daniels Island in South Carolina.

I would also like to extend my deepest appreciation and thanks to the people who participated in this book and made this dream a reality for me. Your kindness and support have helped me grow my career to heights I never thought possible. You are all a driving force in this industry and I want to thank you for providing our readers with the opportunity to learn and become the best at what they do.

Last but not least, I would like to thank the reader. I hope you take this insider information and use it to achieve all your goals and dreams in life. Remember that goals are dreams, so as long as you live your dreams you will always reach your goals. You have the opportunity to do anything you want in life as long as you implement a path for your future. I wish you the best in everything you do.

I have been in the same position as most of our readers. I have spent time stressing where the next deal was coming from, if I was going to remain in this business, overworked and underpaid. It took me five years to eliminate all worries and enjoy my life and career. This is why I wanted to put all this powerful information into one book and give back to you.

Contents

Introduction		vii
Foreword by Dan S. Kennedy		ix
One	Scott Tucker	1
Two	Mike Miget	23
Three	Chris Hurn	43
Four	Jessika Ondrick	75
Five	Tracy Tolleson	95
Six	Brad Cooper	113
Seven	Andy Lockwood	133
Eight	Sue Haviland	155
Nine	Ken Schreiber	175
Ten	Brian Sacks	195
Websites You Need To Know About		217
About the Authors		218

> *"You can make money or you can make excuses, but you can't do both!"*
>
> —Dan Kennedy

Introduction

You have picked up this book because you believe there are better ways to lead your career as a Mortgage Broker. You are interested in knowing how to generate leads, close loans and make more money while working less. This is exactly what you will learn when you read this guide from cover to cover.

The intent of this book is to share with you the insight of the most successful mortgage brokers in this business. I am not talking about the top producers in your office making a decent six-figure income. I am talking about the Gurus who are making high six-figure and seven-figure incomes without any competition. These same gurus have their borrowers paying maximum fees without any objections about costs and rates.

People in our business are trained to discuss rates and fees with their borrowers. This training makes success difficult for anyone without a clear plan. Talking rates and fees is the quickest way to become a commodity to your borrowers and have them leave your iron gate.

The interviews within this book will teach you how to become a specialist and not a generalist. You will know how to attract buyers and keep them coming back to you time and time again. You will learn how to put up an iron gate around your borrowers, so they keep coming back to you and referring you new borrowers. You will discover the little secrets on how to add different revenue streams to your business. You will learn how to get other mortgage brokers to send you business. You will understand how easy a commercial loan can be with the right team and knowledge.

There are plenty of books for borrowers to buy on how to get the right mortgage. Now you have the book that tells you how to get those borrowers and keep them for as long as you want.

There a few characteristics that separate the mortgage brokers from the true mortgage gurus. This book illustrates how the best of our business are doing it. You will read interviews from Scott Tucker, a mortgage marketing genius who makes over $730,000 in fees with him and one assistant. You will read how Mike Miget was once a highly recruited accountant who makes over $2,000,000 in fee income in the mortgage business through effective marketing. You have the opportunity to read what Chris Hurn has to say about the commercial business and how you can make money doing it. Chris is clearly a Commercial Guru who has taken a unique commercial niche and created a company that is moving up the Inc. 500 list every year.

This is an ever-changing business and you need to stay on top of your game to be successful. If you want to do what everyone else is doing, then go ahead and continue to expect the same results. If you want to succeed in this business and develop a career that keeps producing no matter what the market conditions are, you need to absorb everything you can in the next 10 chapters.

To receive your $247 in free bonuses: www.TheInsiderSecretsGift.com

FOREWORD BY DAN S. KENNEDY

'NOT A BOOK TO READ'

Reading a book like this is an exercise in detection.

Like Sherlock Holmes or contemporary sleuths on CSI, you are in search of clues useful in solving the mysteries peculiar and particular to your own mortgage business in specific, business life in general. To draw from, you have a rich and varied collection of ideas and experiences from extraordinarily successful mortgage professionals, brilliantly assembled for you by Nate Kennedy (no relation to me, incidentally).

The people you meet in this book are successful for reasons. Their success is not accidental. I know most of them personally and have been of some significant influence on Scott Tucker, Tracy Tolleson, Mike Miget, Chris Hurn and Brian Sacks. They are different people with different approaches to the business but also with profound commonalities of thought, attitude and behavior. Each individual must ultimately go their own way, as will you. But "your own way" can be built from selected 'clues to success' taken from these different industry, strategy and thought leaders. Certainly your speed and ease of getting wherever you're aimed in this industry will be accelerated and enhanced by what you detect, choose and use from them.

Reading a book like this is a shopping trip to the mall.

Every exceptionally successful person without exception anywhere in recorded history or contemporary life has had and has mentors, 'models', coaches and confidantes. The highest achievers make habit of seeking out and surrounding themselves with individuals with proven, real world experience and expertise—and are very, very willing to pay for it. For 30 years I've been working with "from scratch" millionaires, multi-millionaires and 7-figure income earners in over 150 different fields including yours, and I have yet to encounter one not of this habit, or not cheerfully willing to invest. I have also met many, many, many more people with the opposite habits, meager to embarrassingly meager bank accounts, and little to show for their business activity but excuses for not doing better. And I would quickly make the point that there is no such thing as good or bad economy, slow or fast markets—there are effective people and ineffective people, period.

My friend Jim Rohn tells his story of suggesting that poor people take millionaires out to lunch, to the fanciest and priciest steakhouse, paying for the finest wine and best steak on the menu. "Why", the poor person asks, "should I pay for a millionaire's lunch? He has the million. I don't." Precisely. He knows things you do not know or have stubbornly refused to accept about success and prosperity. You should—as best you can, as

To receive your $247 in free bonuses: www.TheInsiderSecretsGift.com

often as you can—"take a millionaire to lunch." The leaders in this book offer different resources, training programs, coaching programs and classes. Buying them is "taking the millionaire to lunch." You should "shop" this book for the person or persons who resonate with you, who seem most relevant to you, who appear to have the most to offer you—where you are now and where you want to go. Then you should pony up the money to buy their expensive experience. It is a bargain compared to the prices for trial and error drudgery or endless mediocrity and frustration. A little secret: only about 8% of the entire U.S. population is "rich"; 92% not. In your profession, about the same. Most of those in the 8% group got there, in part, by buying their way in—that is, by latching on to one or more of their industry already there and following their lead. Since free advice is usually worth its price and not a penny more, in most of these cases, they've paid for their mentoring. There's been somebody guarding the elevator door and collecting admission; pointing those unwilling to pay toward the 500 flights of stairs accessible to anybody free of charge.

Reading a book like this is an exercise in choice.

By the time you complete it, for it to have value, you need to have made choices. Choices about new ways of thinking about your business to explore, new attitudes to adopt, new strategies to pursue, new guides to hire if you can. If you come away with no such choices firmly made, Nate wasted his time on you, and you wasted your time on this book. That's cold, hard fact.

I've personally written and had over 20 books published in a span of 25 years, read by hundreds of thousands of people, translated and published in 9 different languages and 19 different countries, and recognized by *Inc. Magazine* on their '100

To receive your $247 in free bonuses: www.TheInsiderSecretsGift.com

best business books' list and on *Business Week's* bestseller lists. I am a realist. I know that the vast majority—probably right around 92% of the people—who have read my books manage to go from start to finish without making and subsequently acting on a single new choice in their lives. I have no control over that and accept no responsibility for it. I appreciate the notes and reports of accomplishment I get from the 8% or so who do make and act on new choices. Nate will too, about this book. If you are one of the few who do something, be sure to drop him a note and report in.

This book is about ten different innovators, leaders and 'captains' of your industry. But at the end of the book, at the end of the day, it is really about only one person. You.

Dan Kennedy is internationally recognized as a 'millionaire-maker,' helping people in just about every category of business turn their ideas into fortunes. To learn more about Dan Kennedy and obtain your Most Incredible Free Gift Ever go to:

www.FreeGiftFrom.com/natekennedy

CHAPTER ONE

INTERVIEW WITH SCOTT TUCKER

SCOTT TUCKER is a Mortgage Marketing Genius that has created a phenomenal living doing Subprime Refinances. He has revolutionized a marketing system that generates large revenues, while conducting business in a way that the average Mortgage Broker would never dream about. Scott has swarms of borrowers seeking him out, since he is the obvious Guru in his area. There are not many people making the type of money that Scott is making, while only working 30-35 hours per week. You do not want to miss a single word of this chapter, so read carefully and absorb every word. Let's get right into finding out how Scott Tucker is so successful.

First, how did you end up in the mortgage business?

To make money, I guess. I'm not solely interested in the mortgage business. I'm interested in different things that make a large amount of money. Joan Rivers says, "It's no harder to marry rich than it is to marry poor." It's just a matter of choice, so if you're going to work, you may as well make a lot of money, not a little money. You see folks all the time digging ditches and doing all kinds of crazy things to make money and they're making little bits of money. If they would just turn their attention and efforts in a different direction, they'd make hundreds of thousands of dollars. I'd much rather make a high income than a low income and I think mortgages are a great place to be.

Absolutely! There are many peaks and valleys in our business and people spin their wheels without ever generating high incomes.

There are many ups and downs in the industry as a whole, but there's no reason why any one person in the industry needs to participate in that cycle. That's my belief and I think that's 100 percent the case with the proper marketing and so on. It's also wiser to be a specialist and niche within one area of the mortgage business, rather than being a generalist or chasing your ulcers, or just waiting to see what walks in the door.

Many people in the industry do just sit at the phone hoping it's going to ring instead of going out there and getting that business. They are the same people saying this business is tough. These people are the talkers as opposed to the implementers. You are obviously an implementer, so how have you found your borrowers? Do you use referral sources?

I'm big on not being dependent on others at any time, for any part of your business. Whenever you're dependent on others, it's a weakness and a vulnerability. You ought to be lying awake at night if your business is dependent on referrals from realtors or builders or any one mailing list or any one community group or wherever your leads and referrals are coming from. If you have a single source or only a couple of sources where you're getting things, you'll have problems. You want to fix those problems before they happen, not after, obviously, because then it's too late when suddenly all the money dries up.

My best source of referrals is from past borrowers. Most people would think you need thousands of past borrowers to make that work. But you can have 20, 40, 100 past borrowers and if you work it properly, there's no reason you shouldn't be getting referrals from those folks. I'm also a big proponent of getting repeat business off past borrowers and my system enables people to be able to get three subprime refinances off one new borrower. So one person comes in the door expecting and demanding, really, to do three transactions with you at least. Some people would say, "Isn't that predatory?" or "Isn't that equity stripping?" No, it's not. If there's no benefit to the borrower, we don't do their loan again. But commonly we get people around the 500 credit score with my system and we boost them up to about a 580 score off a first transaction by paying off a bunch of their bills and contesting a couple of things, but not doing too much credit repair work. Then we'll take them from a 580 score up to a 660 in a second transaction, so again there's more benefit to the borrower there. Then we'll take them from the 660 credit score up to about a 740 score or so. So we're turning subprime borrowers into A Paper borrowers.

Now there's a caveat there. They have to learn from their mistakes and about A Paper borrower behavior. However, we can clean them up, get them above 700 with this three-step process even if their behavior is not the greatest. Some people fly right once you've fixed their problems, some people don't and really, you can't feel guilty about that. You do your part; they have to do their part. It's similar to a doctor removing a tumor and then you go and smoke another pack of cigarettes. So you can't control what people are going to do, you can only do your part. If you do your part to the best of your ability, there's no reason why you shouldn't be paid well and there's no reason you shouldn't help them a second time. If you pull a past borrower file from a year or two ago, and look at their credit today—say there's no prepayment penalty—if you pull their credit today you'll see that they refinanced with somebody else because you've not been in contact with that past borrower. So we also have a past borrower retention system that keeps in constant contact with them automatically so we don't need to do a bunch of grunt work. There's a couple-step process and month in, month out, they're automatically hearing from you and that causes repeat business and end referrals from the past borrower list.

You focus your business around subprime borrowers and turning them into A Paper borrowers through multiple deals. These days so many brokers out there do not even want to touch a subprime deal. It amazes me that they look at it being harder instead of being more profitable.

I find myself putting less time on subprime deals than on A Paper deals. When I turn them from a subprime borrower to an A Paper borrower, I never actually give them an A Paper loan because the loans are so time-consuming. They're oftentimes not that much more beneficial than a subprime loan. It's usually more hassle than the borrower wants to put up with and more hassle than I want to put up with and I can get them 99 percent of the results that the A Paper loan can get them. Keep in mind that even though we're boosting their credit scores, many people with 700 credit scores are not "A Paper." You have self-employed people, people with past bankruptcies, past foreclosures. They don't have two month's reserves; whatever the story is, they're not A Paper. We'll get them close, but again, if they can really straighten out their behavior and save some money, and do this and that, then yes, they'll become A Paper borrowers. Generally what I do to simplify my business is after I have them cleaned up to where they're really sparkling clean, which some of them do with their own behaviors, others need the three transactions. When I find that I can no longer help them with subprime loans, I'll refer them to a fellow here in Chicago who's an A Paper broker. In return, he refers customers to me, and is the only other professional that does so. I refer him my people that become A Paper or occasionally I'll get somebody that falls out of the sky who's sparkling clean. I'll send them over to him. He doesn't like to do subprime deals so he sends his subprime deals to me. So that's a good relationship. But I never have to do the kinds of loans that I don't like doing.

That touches on the networking. You partnered up with somebody that actually allows you to refer back and forth clients in your respective niches.

Yes, but you have to view anything that comes from networking as gravy because you can't depend on it. A guy could be hit by a truck tomorrow; he could decide he doesn't like you anymore. He could get out of the business. You don't know what could happen, so you don't want to be dependent on another person. You don't want to be dependent on a single system. You want to have a diversified marketing funnel.

Yes, your marketing funnel is diversified and there's some referral related business from the networking you do as well.

I don't recommend relying on networking alone but yes, it can complement your kind of marketing structure and diversity does lead to stability so that's an important aspect that people forget. Many people in our business end up going in to a feast or famine thing. They got into this business by jumping in to A Paper in the middle of a refi boom and then they don't have a plan for once the party's over. That's one big reason; if you're just joining the business now, don't get into an A Paper refi boom. I know we don't have a refi boom presently but that's the worst, that's the biggest commodity. There's no differentiation. You have no leverage. You have no story to tell in your marketing campaign. There's no way that you're a guru. You're just another loan officer. You're just like the guy in the DiTech commercial who has to buy people chicken dinners so he can get them to talk to him. They're offering $400 flat fees or no fees or free appraisals or we'll pay you to do your loan. It's ridiculous. Why put up with that? In Massachusetts, I believe there's a four percent cap on fees. So you're getting four points in the front. No YSP, no prepayment penalty; here in Illinois I'm getting five points with the state cap; same thing, all in the front, no YSP, no prepayment penalty. The borrowers do not question my fees. They just go happily along because of my system, which conditions them and makes them totally accept the way I do business.

In other states I've got folks, Tennessee, Nebraska, different states that don't have caps, Missouri, my members are getting 7.99 points in the front. They don't have to earn it on YSP if they don't choose and they don't have to take prepayment penalties from lenders. I have lenders that go down to 500 credit score. I have lenders who go below that so there's a much more exciting place to operate because you're no longer a commodity loan officer. And you can't get these giant fees…people who are A Paper borrowers who think their stuff doesn't stink. You can certainly get them from people who are 500, 700, above 700 score who are in some way or another scratched and dented.

The A Paper borrower always believes they should get the best deal out there and they beat you up on everything and sometimes walk for a $100 difference.

Do you really want to get your stuff kicked in every day? If you have to wear a cup to work, you have a problem and you need to fix it. That's just fine, but life's too short. I don't want to live like that. I hope you don't want to either. There's just no reason for all that.

Mortgage brokers also struggle to have strong, consistent pipelines. They have a good month and then follow it up with a bad month. What do you recommend people do to keep those pipelines strong?

When you use the phrase, "pipeline," it makes me think of one thing that I don't want to get into, but many people are enamored with what a genius they are in the matter of how much volume they're doing. Loan volume, well, loan volume you can't take to the bank.

No, I'm talking fees.

I know, but people will also get all wrapped up in how many loans they're doing. You know, "I'm doing 100 loans this month." Well, who cares? Again, we're working on fees here; that's what we ought to be working on. I'm interested in getting the biggest fee for the work, not for not doing anything but the least number of loans and the biggest fees possible per loan so that you're making a big income doing five loans a month, seven loans a month, however many you want to do. Some members of my program do four loans a month and they're getting huge incomes. I have people doing anywhere from $100,000, $200,000 a year income that are just slackers, I would call them. It's quite common for people in my program to be getting $400,000, $500,000, $600,000 a year incomes, just them and one processor. They usually work about 35 hours a week. I have a couple of people that are almost up to a million dollars a year who are working a bit harder. Actually, I have one person who is well over a million but he was already a psychotic workaholic before I got him. He was already successful but he just had a $350,000 month, but he was already doing $100,000-plus a month anyway. So he got a bit better with my program. So I take, I guess what I would call slackers and losers if that's not too harsh a term—it's not because anybody's really a loser, it's because they don't know what to do, the right way, the way that nobody else teaches. I take slackers and losers, turn them into winners, take winners and turn them into bigger winners. There comes a point where no matter how much harder you work, you can't get to the next level by yourself.

That is exactly why I decided to join your coaching program. It is great to be with like-minded people. I actually followed your program for a year before I joined. It still upsets me to think about all the money I gave up by not jumping on this opportunity earlier. How do you recommend people get involved in your coaching program?

Well obviously, you join the program and read the fax that has a bit of coaching in the first portion of the fax. The middle portion of the fax is a fast action list and I think

To receive your $247 in free bonuses: www.TheInsiderSecretsGift.com

there's something like 41 different items that I ask you to do. You don't have to do all of them, but it's clear when you have the fax which ones you should concentrate on. Some of them are as simple as making a phone call to a vendor. Some of them are as simple as going into one of my websites and clicking here and there and getting something accomplished that way; e-mailing or calling a couple vendors. There are a couple of recordings you set up on phone lines and stuff like that but it's not really too challenging at all. I think you could knock it out in your spare time over a week or certainly during the weekend you could get it all done.

You just paint by the numbers; I wanted to make my system easy. I built my system for myself for my own business. Once I had it I showed it to Dan Kennedy—people should know who Dan Kennedy is, if they don't they can go to askdankennedy.com. I showed Dan Kennedy what I was doing in a coaching meeting, because I have a coach as well, and he said, "This is unbelievable. You ought to be teaching other people how to do this." So I created area-exclusive programs. You have your area, I have my area. My guy in Omaha has Omaha; my guy in Knoxville, Tennessee has Knoxville, Tennessee, and so on. Everybody gets their own area and we end up with a mastermind group. That's another benefit of the coaching; people find they have a network of people on their side who are also doing the same stuff. So you join my program and now you have 150 guys to work with that are all cooperative. You just paint by the numbers.

The last part of the fax shows the schedule of our coaching calls and our different events. Every year in January, we have a Scott Tucker's Birthday Party. So this year it's Scott Tucker's 34th Birthday Party and we're going to Puerto

To receive your $247 in free bonuses: www.TheInsiderSecretsGift.com

Rico for that. Then we'll have three other member meetings a year and usually a seminar or two each year as well. There's just so much support and so much reinforcement; we have a Google group that's restricted to member use only. There are so many different ways you're supported, I don't see any reason anyone shouldn't succeed with it and I think that's why there's a high rate of success for my members as well.

People need to implement your system, instead of just sitting around waiting for the business to come to them.

It's *Groundhog Day* and you know people do it. The definition of insanity is to do the same thing and expect a different result. I think people get into a rut. At first they learn to do what everybody else is doing, which is just idiotic because the average residential loan officer in the United States makes $65,000 a year. I don't know why you got in the mortgage business, but I'll tell you one reason I did not get into the business and that's to make $65,000 a year.

Oh no, I got in it because I was able to make a lot of money.

If you want to make $65,000 a year, just go become a schoolteacher. It would be probably a lot less stressful and more vacation time, as far as the three months off. I don't know what I would do with three months. If you want to work a couple hours a day and do that, that's fine. Not to say that you need to overwork in the mortgage business either, once you have a system. Like I said, just about all my guys are part time and doing a few hundred thousand dollars a year. But I would just go work for the power company or something and turn your brain off and read meters or something if you just want to make 55, but I like something a little bit more exciting than that.

To receive your $247 in free bonuses: www.TheInsiderSecretsGift.com

I'm with you on that. I don't like turning the day off. **My mind is constantly running and thinking of new opportunities and creating different ideas but I guess that's what separates many of us from people who just want to have that nine-to-five job.**

It goes back to what I was saying: if you're going to do what everybody else has done, you're going to get what everyone else has. When you go to your continuing ed. classes or your mortgage broker association, you see all the guys pull up with the car that has the duct tape on the bumper and he's on his cell phone nonstop, kissing every realtor's butt because he has to. He's cutting fees, he's calling title companies asking them to cut their fees, he's working on this close. When I have to spend a day in the continuing ed. class, I sit there quietly, peacefully at ease. I know that money's coming in from my mortgage business without me freaking out and being a nut case.

I like to call the people you're referring to 'the 30K millionaires.' They drive the nice car but that's about all they can afford as they rent a place and they're not living their life as it should be.

The guy with the shiniest cell phone is usually the guy that's the most broke. You have guys in the continuing ed. classes with their chargers plugged into the walls. So really, you have to have control over your time in your life, your lifestyle and most people don't, and that's not at all what my goal is.

You touched on one thing earlier that I want to come back to. You mentioned the importance of having a coach. Do you think having a coach is important in succeeding and useful to growing your career?

To receive your $247 in free bonuses: www.TheInsiderSecretsGift.com

It's enormously useful. The difference between when I didn't have a coach and now that I do is a ton of money. When you have a coach, you have somebody who sees your potential even when you don't see it. That's useful because many of us view our potential based on our past and our present. Even when we imagine the future, we can't see the potential. A coach can see beyond that and help you break through what you think are these barriers. Having a coach has exploded my income. I don't even know what more to say about it other than it's the most important thing in the world. You see it in sports. We don't have NFL teams that go out there without coaches. Imagine the chaos that would occur if we had a team walk on the field without a coach and the other team did have a coach. Yet people treat their business as if they don't need a coach and it's just ridiculous.

Along with coaching, what type of stuff do you read daily that helps you progress your career and would be great advice for our readers to go ahead and pick up?

Some important books are *Think and Grow Rich* by Napoleon Hill, *Psychology: The Influence of Persuasion* by Robert Cialdini, Robert Ringer's book *To Be or Not To Be Intimidated?*, anything by Dan Kennedy, Larry Steinmetz' *How to Sell at Prices Higher than your Competitors*, *Psycho-Cybernetics* by Dr. Maxwell Maltz. Those are probably the most important that come to mind right now but Dan's got about 11 different books you can read as well, *No BS* books, which are all excellent.

I've read a few you mentioned and I've actually just picked up a collection of the Dan Kennedy books and have been getting into them…it's amazing how they just suck you in. The way he thinks about things and explains how much time you can save

To receive your $247 in free bonuses: www.TheInsiderSecretsGift.com

and how you can succeed by doing things differently than your competitors. It's amazing how it can get you different places as opposed to following the rat race.

Exactly—information is the most valuable thing there is. Most people never take any advantage of it. You see people in lines for Playstation 3s and shooting each other and wrestling in line and beating each other up and getting hauled off to jail, yet you don't see anybody lined up outside of the library or the Barnes & Noble. My Barnes & Noble locks the restroom but they keep the books unlocked. I think you could take 10 books inside your coat and just walk out the door and nothing would happen. But they've got the restroom locked up so the homeless guy doesn't wash his armpits in it. This makes no sense, lock up the bathroom but don't lock up the information, yet everybody's trying to get into the restroom, nobody is trying to get into the books. People go into the Barnes & Noble just to use the bathroom, not to look at any books. They just go in there to get Starbucks but they don't look for any information. All the information in the bookstore is useful but what's amazing to me is that they never enter the Business and Self-Improvement and Real Estate and those sections. They never go there. They want to read the next novel about something that never happened. It's ridiculous.

More people should educate themselves through reading.

My brain is my own entertainment center, I guess I would think of it. Many people don't; they want to shut their brain off and never use it and take the easy way out. Homer Simpson takes the easy way out too but you see what happens with him. He never gets ahead and you know it's another beer, another day at the power plant and another fight

To receive your $247 in free bonuses: www.TheInsiderSecretsGift.com

with the wife and the kid kicks you in the shin. They never improve their lives because they never use their brains. They go along and are puppets to what their puppet masters want them to do, whether it's the government or their boss or whatever.

I was listening to one of your informational CDs and you're talking about how people may go broke but intellectually they never can.

What's funny about that too is many people are intellectually poor currently, but they'll look at the shiny object, the new car or the new whatever that they want to buy. Often they'll look at cars rather than real estate; just silliness like that. They'll want a doodad but they don't want to have any net worth. They don't want to have any intellectual kind of net worth. They don't want to have any intellectual ability. They just want the shiny object and they're so immersed in the instant gratification present they don't ever look at what tomorrow is going to be like. If they don't plan for tomorrow, tomorrow is going to end up being whatever it's going to end up being. People let life do it to them rather than doing it to life. They don't plan their lives. They just take whatever comes. They have their hand out like a beggar and if they get a penny that's one thing, if they get a $20 bill it's another thing or $100 bill, but they have no control over whether they get a penny or a $100 bill. If you have no control over it, well I'll tell you what you're going to get. You're going to get squat or a penny and that's just insane. I hate to see people at less than their full potential, but most people are stubbornly stuck there.

That and some people feel they're entitled to things.

If you have an entitlement mentality, and you actually have no legitimate reason you should be rewarded for whatever it is that you're doing or not doing, that is a huge vulnerability. One day you'll no longer receive that entitlement. There's no logical reason why you should receive an entitlement, and you may one day no longer receive it.

With your success, do you have people that look at you for handouts?

Anybody who views me as their piggybank, I kick out the door. There's no room for vampires in my life. Also, it shows a poor quality person if somebody expects you to give them everything and then to give you nothing—that's just ridiculous. Somebody who has no sense of the law of reciprocity in their life and in their dealings with people is a poor quality person. You really can't have them around. Any deal where you get rich later, where they'll pay you out of their next such and such over the next 10 months. Well, it's really cash in the barrel anytime you expect to get money in arrears; you're going to get money in arrears or not at all.

True. It brings me to the reality that if your friends aren't succeeding, or succeeding with the goals you have, you need to find new friends.

I'm sure it sounds harsh to everybody and mean-spirited and whatever else. One of my best friends growing up is a third-shift worker at a dairy plant in Lansing, Michigan. He sleeps on milk crates, third shift and he punches in, punches out. He does his 40 hours, gets whatever pension they give him that can be stolen from him at anytime, of course. He gets like $13 an hour and he goes home to his high school sweetheart who he married, and they had a child together.

To receive your $247 in free bonuses: www.TheInsiderSecretsGift.com

He didn't plan anything really. He just let it all happen to him. He married a girl who he used to fight with in high school so they still fight today. They went and had a kid so they complicate the situation even more. He took the first job he found out of high school and is still making the same income he made when he was 18 years old or just slightly above with the union-scale pay raise. The day that they start processing all the milk for Lansing, Michigan in Grand Rapids instead or something happens like that, there is no security. People look for security all the time and they end up giving up all security by trying to give away all the responsibility for their life to other people. Anytime you give away responsibility like that, you're going to be punched for it. The only certainty he has in his life is $13 an hour and he doesn't even have that. If you teach yourself how to make $100,000, $500,000, $1 million this year, once you've taught yourself that, you can't unlearn it and it can't be taken away from you. Even if, for some reason, mortgages go away tomorrow, those marketing and sales skills—especially the marketing—can be applied to a different business. There's no reason you ever need be hungry again.

You can always take the knowledge you've gained alone and put it into different areas. Increase and generate revenue in other aspects. We should get back on the mortgage side for our readers here. What do you recommend to mortgage brokers that chase a deal and don't know when to give it up?

Here's an analogy that just about everybody understands, whether they're male or female. If you're no longer single, you can still remember the time that you were, high school or whatever. Remember a time when you pursued someone, they said no and you kept pursuing them, what did that do? Well it demonstrated that you were of lower status. It demonstrated that you needed the deal. It demonstrated that you didn't deserve the deal. It demonstrated you were desperate. It made the other party run the other way even faster than they were already running. What did it do to your quality, the way you thought of yourself? It destroyed your own self-image. Now every woman can think about when she was on the other end of that and exactly why she didn't like the guy—because he chased the deal and needed the deal, didn't have anything else in his pipeline. It's simple psychology.

I say again, the book by Robert Cialdini *Psychology: The Influence of Persuasion,* can explain it a good deal. You cannot operate in a chase position like that and succeed. It's impossible. One of Dan Kennedy's books, *No BS Sales Success,* has a chapter that's dedicated to what he calls "Take away selling." Take away selling is exactly what you need to be using. It's funny; you can actually make take away selling work with your direct mail. People don't perceive that you're actually chasing them verbally if they just get a letter in the mail; they don't perceive it as you chasing them if you do it correctly, like the way my stuff is set up.

Customers perceive themselves as initiating; see, I only deal with people who call me or apply online or whatever. I don't deal with anybody who doesn't chase me first. So I might mail a couple thousand sales letters and get however many calls back but I'm not dealing with any kind of sales resistance or reluctance or any of that crap or anybody who hasn't already raised their hand and say, "Yeah I want that." Once you've applied your sales skills only to the people who want to be sold, your life is 100 percent different.

To receive your $247 in free bonuses: www.TheInsiderSecretsGift.com

Most people spend their time trying to convince others that they want to be sold when they don't. They say, "Well no, I don't want to be sold, get away." They just chase harder and that psychology kicks in that, "Uh-oh, this guy needs this deal too much. He probably can't make his car payment if he doesn't get my money. I don't want to be anywhere near him." On the other hand, I convey a totally different feeling and so do my members when they use my marketing.

Definitely; it is wild that people act like they need that deal when in all honesty the borrower needs the money. Chasing people definitely lowers your ROI. What type of return on investment are your members seeing?

I just did a teleseminar the other night for folks who are not yet in my program. We had people on the call and I didn't know what their numbers were going to be. Their numbers were between 20 and 50 times cost on their mail. Then I had a person that did my door hangers, and he got some ridiculous thing like 173 times the cost of the printing of the door hangers plus the hanging of the door hangers and no, he doesn't go hang them himself. It's a copyrighted piece, written by me, filed at the Library of Congress in D.C. We have protected all that marketing so there's nobody else in his area that can use it. When you're getting 20 times cost under direct mail, 50 times cost with direct mail, 173 times cost on your door hangers and all these things are being done for you. We have hand-addressed direct mail; we're not hand addressing it, that's being done for us by the vendor.

A thousand letters is about $1,000 spent, but you can spend that on your credit card and then a month later, you got your money and you pay the credit card off. So if you spent $1,000, made $20,000, which is 20 times the cost, then you made a profit of $19,000 in one month. People should be excited about that, not afraid of it. One thousand dollars is the same amount of money that a bankruptcy attorney would charge you to go bankrupt. Would you rather go bankrupt or would you rather make $19,000 this month?

That's all training the mind to think that way and often people think, "Well, that's a lot of money to spend," as opposed to, "Look at the money I'm losing out on."

It's a lot of money, and $19,000 in a month is a lot of money to make in net profit for most people, too. Many people work three or four months to make that much if they even make that much.

How fast are people closing their deals from the moment they drop a direct mail piece from your system?

From the day you drop the mail you should have closed deals in three to four weeks. The deal that closed in three weeks with the recession will have them inside of a month.

What type of things did you struggle or fail at to get to this point today?

I don't know that I ever failed per se, but I don't like pain a lot. I mean pain as far as mental, emotional, physical, not being able to eat, can't put gas in the car, got to worry about the landlord and all that kind of stuff. I don't like that kind of discomfort. When I was growing up, we didn't really have the amount of money that we needed all the time. And I never wanted to be like that again. It's not so much failure, but just grunting it out trying to sell rather than trying to market is a huge mistake. I got smart in a hurry that the opportunity is in the direct response marketing of the thing, not in being better at doing the thing. You want to be the best loan officer. You want to be the loan officer who's making the most money. So rather than going to umpteen classes on PMI and this and that and RESPA again, whatever your state requires of you. Going to classes every week or going to all the cocktail parties that the association might have. That's going on and on about being a better loan officer, but it doesn't make you any more money. What makes you more money is honing your sales skills. Something that everybody ought to get a hold of is Tom Hopkins' *Low Profile Selling* CDs and you get them at TomHopkins.com. So hone your sales skills but then beyond that, the best salesman working on the worst prospect, using a method that does not allow the use of take away selling, is a total waste of time. So the best salesman spending five hours, or five minutes an hour working with a good prospect and another 55 minutes an hour working with terrible prospects, what's the sense in that? There's 12 times the money to be made if you'll just fix your process and have marketing feed you leads rather than you chasing leads. So right away, I learned that I had to get smart about direct response marketing and that's exactly what I did.

There are people that stress out over this business because they're chasing those deals and don't have those deals coming to them. You know the ups and downs in the business. You created this system so the mortgage business may be up, it may be down, but the system is always consistent and getting business depending on how you bring that in. What have you done to keep yourself focused on your alternate goals?

The business as a whole may go up and down but that's taken care of by people coming and leaving the business. So there's no reason for any one person to suffer when they've got their marketing and sales systems figured out. But I stay focused on my goals by not living in the past. Often people look at where they grew up, how they grew up, who their parents were, what their parents did, what's the most your dad ever made. They set their expectations for themselves by their parents or by the peer group that they used to have.

I choose to be around people who are like-minded, who are at my level or above for the most part. I don't seek to associate with people who don't have my goals in common. You know there's a saying that if you took your five closest friends and you took all their incomes and averaged them out, that average income would be close to your income. So if you get your five friends together, each guy makes about $50,000 a year, there's a good chance that's what your income is as well. It doesn't mean you have to disown your friends, but you should be careful about limiting your time exposed to family, friends, anybody who doesn't have like goals. Again, it might sound harsh, but you know this is about self-improvement. This is about spending more time with people who are at your level and above. It's not all about money, it's about your quality of life, the quality of person you are; the quality of person you are goes beyond your income. It goes to charity and different things, with time and money and family life. The way you see the world is oftentimes influenced by your peer group so much that most people never realize that. It's so important that you hang out with the right people and get rid of the people that are negative influences.

My mom always told me that you are who you hang with.

That's right.

I know you have plenty of stuff going on throughout your day. So just to hear it from you, all of our readers are asking where's the best place for mortgage brokers if they want to turn around their careers and take control of their lives and take control of their business? What's the best way to contact you to get set up with your services?

> I ask that they go to MortgageMarketingGenius.com to become familiar with my system; there's a whole bunch of information there. There are income proofs, so you know that I'm not just a blowhard, copies of my checks, pictures of me when I was little. I give you so much info on me that you're sick of me by the time you're done reading it. There's also information on my members all across the country and in Canada. There are lists of the areas that are not available and then you can figure out if your area is available from that list. There are audio testimonials and print testimonials and copies of checks from my members. There's so much proof there and different things that you can be sure that what I'm saying is for real, because I know many people probably think it's a bunch of BS after reading this interview. Also, they can listen to a free three-hour teleseminar on the site. So go through that site and learn a whole bunch of stuff you haven't learned before and think a way you haven't thought before and it's not all just a big rah-rah session. Quite a few things need to be learned that most people don't know.

Make sure you check in with Scott Tucker and keep up with the new, innovative things he is doing for our industry.

Chapter Two

Interview with Mike Miget

MIKE MIGET is the Mortgage Marketing Maverick who is called the 10-Million-Dollar-Man of Mortgage Marketing. He rediscovered a forgotten financial secret and used it to repackage his mortgage business to bring in over $2,000,000 per year. Mike has generated a marketing process that has more than one stream of income. The process is so unbelievable that people are lining up to work with him without Mike ever making an outbound cold call. As you can imagine, this has helped Mike live the life he wants while making more money than the average Mortgage Broker can imagine.

Thank you for sharing your insight with us.

Today, if you're going to be serious about the business and make a career out of it and really want to achieve what most people would call success or do really well at it, you've got to be more than just a traditional loan officer. You have to think of yourself more than just that because there is a loan officer or mortgage broker on just about every street corner in every city, in every state. Territories that used to be the main hunting ground for mortgage brokers like subprime and alternative-type mortgages, more and more banks and bigger lenders are starting to move into those areas, too. You have to be more than that nowadays.

It's one thing that I strive to do every day.

Many people are attracted to this business because they hear about the money, they hear about the easy money, and it's mortgages. Rates are X, you can get them Y, and Y is lower than X. So, it makes sense. People think they are selling them something when they do that, but they're not; they're just a product provider, or what I would call a replaceable cog in the wheel. One loan officer is as good as the next. They get into the business without really having a good understanding of what it is or actually supposed to be doing out there or what the realm of possibility is to be doing out there. They come in under a certain set of circumstances for a particular reason, such as like a refi boom that we've had over the last several years; and then when those conditions cease to exist and their business dries up, they don't know what to do.

There was a refinance boom when I got in the business. It was great to be in it, but I realized it wasn't going to be there forever.

I got started in this business way back in 1992 when I was fresh out of college. Before I got into the business, I actually went to college to be an accountant; I worked for an accountant/estate planner/attorney all through college. Then when I got out, I had actually been groomed to take a job with one of the big six accounting firms back at the time when there were six of them. I had done personal and corporate taxes, and I was being groomed to move into the personal financial services divisions for one of the accounting firms at the time. You go to college, you spend all that time moving towards a certain goal. I learned quickly that that's not what I wanted to do with my life, so I quickly got out of that.

I frequently talk about my background in accounting because it's that background that enabled me to have the foundation that ultimately formed the basis for the system that I apply to borrowers and their debt nowadays. When I got out of accounting and moved into the mortgage business, I got into the business the same way that many people do. I had a friend that was doing it; he was talking about all the money that he was making and could be made, and he got me into the business. When I did that, I learned the business the same way that everyone else did, which was from him, which he had learned from other people that were in the business. You end up doing things the way that they're supposed to be done, or what industry norms would say, things that you learn about when you go to the association meetings.

When everybody's copying everybody else and learning from each other in that type of an environment, it has a name; and we call it marketing incest. The longer that goes on, the dumber everybody gets; so when one guy copies another guy, copies another guy, copies another guy, eventually the copy of the copy of the copy isn't quite as good as what you originally started with.

That's how I learned to do the business; and I moved in during the refi boom, so I learned how to take people from 9 and 10 percent rates, and we were taking them down to 8s. We would find people who had finance company loans at 12, or 13, or 14 percent; we would move them into what were the beginnings of like a formal subprime market at the time. We'd move them into like 9 and 10 percent loans because back then, there was a big gap between what the banks would lend and what the finance companies would lend, and there was a group of people there in the middle.

You think it's a lot easier these days to finance people?

Yes. There's money available today under conditions that didn't exist 15 years ago. This stuff we take for granted—100 percent financing or 125 percent financing—that didn't exist back then. I remember when we first got going in this; somebody had to have perfect credit in order to get 80 or 85 percent loan to value. Today, if you can get somebody at 80 or 85, it seems like these people have a lot of equity because there's still a lendable portion there; but we're talking about what I would call collateral-based lending. The lenders would require a relatively significant amount of equity in the property before they would lend.

You mentioned earlier that we need to be more than a loan officer. What is the business we are in as opposed to just being a loan officer?

A loan officer really is just a job title; it came from the banking industry where if you work at a bank, everybody has a title. Tellers are VPs. Well, there's a person that would sit in a corner at a desk, and his title was chief loan officer. He's the one who decided who got loans, so that's where that name came from. It's just a job title and doesn't really define what loan officers do. I think the mortgage business is a crappie business to the end. I say that not from the perspective that what we do is crappie, but if you think of yourself as being in the mortgage business and that defines what you do in terms of a mortgage, in our case that's the product that we provide, you're going to have a rough go of it because mortgages are essentially a commodity. The mortgage that I get somebody is the same one that the guy across the street can get, is the same one that Countrywide or DiTech, or whomever you want to talk about, can get.

There really isn't much, if any, differentiation when you define what you do in terms of that product. What I say is instead of defining yourself or what you do through the product that you provide, just think of that as a tool that you use to deliver what it is you really sell. For example, this is much easier to see in terms of when you're talking about a purchase money transaction. It's not much of a stretch to convince somebody that when you're doing a purchase money loan for a borrower, it's not the mortgage that they're buying; in their mind, they're buying a house. Then the mortgage becomes a necessary evil, so to speak, for getting that home. They've got in their mind, "I'm buying this house."

Well, when you move that over into a refinance transaction, we don't have that home there anymore. So, people tend to focus on buying a loan. They're doing the loan because they're getting a lower rate or getting cash back or something like that, but you really have to think of it in terms of what is this loan doing for the people? Why are they doing this transaction? What's the reason for them to do this? Then the sale becomes about that, whatever that outcome is, whatever those groups of benefits are, the emotional benefits behind them taking out that mortgage, just like there's a huge emotional benefit to someone buying a home.

It's great for everyone that isn't like every other cookie cutter person that talks about rates and fees; you talk about the benefits and advantages. There probably had to be some stuff that led you to this. What were some of the things that helped you learn all this and get to the point of realizing that you're not just the loan officer, unless you just came into the business automatically and were like that?

Oh, no, no, no, no, no. I wouldn't even have wanted it to be that easy because I wouldn't be able to appreciate it. There's benefit to the journey of having gone through all of this. The simple answer is the hows, the whys, and the wheres; I mean, I've considered myself at one time to be a failure in the business. It's the way that everyone comes to find or make progress or breakthroughs in what they're doing. That thing that they're doing has to either not be working or be failing or something in order to stimulate them to go looking for a better way…specifically, people won't go fixing something that's not broken. If we go back, I remember I got started in the business in '92 during a refi boom. Fast forward to 1994; that year was my first refi bust. That refi bust was a lot worse than what we are experiencing now in terms of the speed of which it came on and the differential and the rates that we experienced.

At that time, I remember doing conventional-type loans, upwards of 9 ½-10 percent early that year. They had moved up from like the 7 percent range seemingly overnight; it was over a course of a week or so. If you didn't have your pipeline locked in, then forget it. You were going to lose whatever you didn't have locked in because they had gone up that fast.

Up to that point, I had been selling rates and fees; or what I thought I was selling was rates and fees, and that business dried up, and I had to find something else to sell. That's when I began developing what it is that I do today, so it had its roots back in 1994 up through now and then moving on into the future. If we fast forward to the year 2000, and I won't bore you with all the ugly details, but that was another refi bust year when most of the business, as most loan officers know it, had dried up.

I came to a realization at that point. When you keep returning to a certain situation over and over and over again, I had a great system for doing loans. I was a great technician. I was a great loan officer; I thought I knew everything about the business, but I realized I didn't know anything about how to get the business. I had a great loan system, but I didn't have the marketing to go with it. So if you don't have clients, if you don't have lead generation flow, you can be the smartest person in the world, but you're still going to fail.

That's the reality that I found myself in at that time, and I went through the emotional trauma that everybody in that situation goes through and what many loan officers are experiencing today—the thought of getting out of the business. I hated it because I was failing, and it was hard, and it was tough; and I didn't know what to do to fix it because up to that point, I had been a technical-type person. I probably leaned more towards the processing and underwriting side of the business and the approach that I took to it rather than a true sales and marketing approach.

Just remember my background was accounting; in fact, seven years ago when I was going through that and up to that point, I probably wouldn't even have been able to do a call like this today because I didn't have the skills to really talk and present. I wasn't strong in those areas. But, I could look around at other people; and I knew that there were still people making a whole crapload of money in the business. I knew it was still possible. I just knew that I didn't know what I needed to know in order to make it work. That's when I found Dan Kennedy; I got something reinforced in me that I had already known, but it helps to have somebody tell you about it. Marketing and learning how to do it is the most important thing, and if you're not number one at what you do, you need to reinvent what you do so you are. What that means is you're going to have to go out and reengineer your business to suit you.

I knew there were aspects about the business that I didn't like; I knew there were things that I didn't want to be a part of anymore. He was the first person that really said hey, you know what? You can have whatever kind of business you want; you just have to engineer it and build it to produce that outcome. I sat down and made a list of all the things that I liked and all the things that I didn't like. He talked a lot about niching and focusing on a certain thing and really putting some thought into whom it is you go after when you're doing your marketing because up to that point, like many brokers today, I was just taking anything and everything.

I thought of homeowners as my market, and that anybody with a loan was a prospect. I was in the loan business, swapping out one loan for another and all the traditional reasons, such as cash out, or debt consolidation, or locking an ARM into a fixed, or whatever people wanted, and the reasons that they did loans, and that was where it was. That's fine; but you would find yourself doing loans with all kinds of different lenders, and you constantly have to figure out a way to do a loan. It really wasn't conducive to doing many loans or creating something that was systematic. You know, when you're a jack-of-all-trades, you're the master of none.

That's true. You see many people out there that are the jack-of-all-trades; they want to do everything for every client.

Yes, they're trying to be, and the reason for this is that they just don't have enough clients in the first place. There's a way to engineer it so that number one, you're driving the type of customer and borrower to you that you want and that you're repelling away the ones that you don't want so that your business can be more streamlined.

Since you've done all that, do you feel that you're selling as hard as you used to, or have your processes helped you only work with people that want to work with you?

You do all that so that you don't have to sell hard; and if you find yourself having to sell hard, that's a tip-off that maybe you're not doing the things you could do up front so that people come to you already predisposed to buy. That's a function of good marketing; there's a certain part of the process that can be taken over by marketing. Information can be transmitted to prospects prior to you having to do any manual labor for them. That helps do a system sort on who your client is going to be.

Right now, somebody puts either an ad in the paper, or they'll buy a lead from a lead provider; the first thing they want to do is get on the phone and start selling the person. Although that's fine and it works, it's manual-labor intensive, so it begins to limit the number of people that they can communicate with monthly, which is going to limit the amount of income that they can make. When you mix that with talking to anybody and everybody that calls you, it's a

To receive your $247 in free bonuses: www.TheInsiderSecretsGift.com

recipe for disaster, financially at least, because you're going to find yourself spinning your wheels a lot talking to people that you shouldn't be talking to.

You can use marketing, you can use ads and display ads, sales letters, websites, e-mails, and stuff like that to educate or transmit preliminary information to your prospect. That takes over part of that manual selling process. If you can tell them something in a sales letter, you don't have to sit there and tell it to them for the first time on the telephone. When they get that information, and now you're talking to them, they've already been affected by it; so you move from someone that's selling into a reinforcement position, reinforcement of that information. If they were opposed to what you're talking about, you probably wouldn't be on the phone with them in the first place. You can shorten the amount of time spent, manual labor spent on them, by using leverage in your marketing.

How do you work with people, even though they are sold on you before you work with them? You still probably get the rates and fees question, since that is how people are trained to view mortgages. How do you diffuse those questions?

See, borrowers have been taught that; they don't just pop out of the room being rate and fees and stuff. That is what they're taught. They're taught that by all the marketing and advertising that's out there that advertises rates, free appraisals, no closing costs, and stuff like that. In fact, I was driving past a local bank in town yesterday, and right there on the window, in that fluorescent paint or whatever they have, home equity loans, no closing costs. If I see that, let's just say I'm a regular Joe Schmo driving by, and I'm thinking that hey, you know what, I might need a mortgage loan or home equity loan or whatever, and I see that. I go in there, and I ask for one. What do you think I'm going in there for? I mean the bait that they use to attract me was no closing costs; so obviously, naturally, they almost have to expect that's what I'm going to want when I go in there. That's what attracted me in there in the first place; that's what happens to many mortgage companies and loan officers.

When they're doing their marketing, they're unknowingly attracting the wrong people in the wrong way. The way that you get around that, you can do objection handling and learn sales technique and all that. I prefer to use a different bait to attract them in the first place; so that when you initially encounter them, they're not showing up on your doorstep because you have the lowest rate advertised in the paper. Or, you're going to give them a loan for free, or you're going to beat anybody's deal, or whatever; they're showing up there for another reason. I call that marketing to a problem rather than the product. The bank that has the goofy sign in the window, or the mortgage company that has the ad in the paper that lists the rate or whatever trains people, as we know, to shop rates. When they've already decided they need a mortgage, they slip into mortgage-buying mode. They know how to do that, which is to ask rates and fees; then they'll start their shopping process.

That's not the right prospect for me; that's not the prospect that I want to spend time with. We'll do our marketing to address or attract people that have a certain problem, and the solution to that problem is something that I can deliver via a tool that we call a mortgage. They're not showing up to buy a mortgage; they're showing up to get a problem solved, and that's really key to getting out of that rate and fee environment where that's all they want to talk about.

I had a call this morning with a potential borrower that I picked up from my direct marketing. She had credit card debt with high rates and wanted me to wipe it away so she didn't have to pay for it. How would you have handled that situation?

That's the proverbial, I want to be on a diet, I want to lose weight, but I want to eat chocolate cake, donuts and chicken wings and drink beer. It might not be possible. That's really the realm of the credit counselors, debt negotiators and bankruptcy people. Those are the 'have your cake and eat it too,' where you can decide that, "Hey, I don't want to pay that debt anymore. I just want it to go away." They can make it go away, but don't think it's going to be any less of a painful process. They're going to go through a lot of trauma. Creditors start to get cranky when they don't get their payments.

That's where I was back during the '90s when I was developing my system and before I had the right sales and marketing thinking. I was still trying to sell mortgages, and you're right. I've been in this situation a thousand times where I had somebody sitting in front of me, and they had what they thought was a good mortgage on their home. Then, they have these credit cards, but they don't want to touch the home in order to do anything with the credit cards. They might be open to doing something with their house; but they have a seven percent rate now, and I would need to dictate a higher rate than what they are paying now. So, they're like, "Well, why would I want to refinance my seven percent into an eight percent just to get rid of my credit cards?" I constantly found myself defending my solution to solve their problem.

At the end of the day, it shouldn't really matter how the solution is delivered as long as it doesn't cause them financial harm and there's a reasonable expectation that they can get the outcome that you're promising them. It really shouldn't matter, but there's an emotional connection between people and their homes and their mortgage because they've been brainwashed into thinking rate, rate, rate, and rate.

It's something that I call managing debt; people have become good managers of their debt. They know how to shop for mortgages, and they know how to get the lowest rate on that, and how to get it free; maybe someday companies wouldn't start paying people to take out mortgages with them. They know how to go shop for the lowest credit card rate, they know how to do balance transfers, and for years, they've known that they can get their car financed for free. They go out, and they've got a five percent mortgage, and they've got zero percent on their car, and they've got zero or one or two on a significant amount of credit card debt, and they're thinking okay, I'm as good as I can be. So, I don't need to mess with this anymore. That's the logical approach to it; but at the end of the day, they're still broke. They don't have any money in the bank, they don't have any emergency funds set aside, they're living paycheck to paycheck, and they're not getting ahead financially.

The next question is, what's the deal here? Why am I not getting ahead? I'm doing everything that I'm supposed to be doing. I have the best deals that I can get on everything; I'm not able to get ahead. That's why instead of managing debt, we focus on eliminating debt because obviously, it would be better if you didn't have the debt rather than having the debt and managing it to death. For most people nowadays, that's the only way that they're going to be able to set money aside and retire. They're not going to be able to save while they're paying debt, paying off credit cards, paying off cars; the rates and the amount of interest that they're paying doesn't have as much to do with it as they think because that's what they've been trained to think. What has more of an impact on the cash flow and the potential benefit of cash flow, is that it could be used for other purposes rather than servicing payments on debt that's going to last 15, 20 or 30 years.

Even with this scenario, it's almost as if they haven't fallen under yet and taken that turn. Some people sit on the brink of their credits. That's okay; they haven't missed payments. They may have had a 30-day here and there, but soon it's just going to be a downward spiral. How do you talk with people that still have that prideful mentality of "I don't need help. I have this, I have that, and that'll never happen to me," but your experience knows that it happens to most people that are in that position.

The simple answer to the question is we don't talk to them because my marketing does not attract them. In order for someone to end up in my funnel, they have to perceive themselves as having a problem. If somebody doesn't perceive themselves as having a problem, or something that needs to be fixed, they're not attracted to me. We try to do as much of that as we can up front to keep away from those people, and they end up not responding because they don't respond to the problem copy.

Now, sometimes people will deep down know that they are either having a problem, or they can see a problem on the horizon, and they'll begin their quest for information because we position ourselves as a source of information for people who are interested in this topic of debt and debt elimination. They will come into the funnel deep down knowing that they're having a problem, but they're not ready to admit it yet. Really all you can do is just point out to them where they're going, and you're pointing out things that they already know, conclusions that they've already drawn. You just have to be in front of them constantly in enough times to where when they finally are ready to make a move, you're the one that they think of.

You stick them on your list of someone that you can still consistently mail to, knowing that in the future, maybe a month, maybe two months, it's going to get to a point where it's just a little bit too much for them to handle. So they come back to you as opposed to you chasing them.

We are constantly mailing a sales presentation because essentially that's what marketing is. Every letter you send out or e-mail or whatever should be some type or have some semblance of a sales presentation to it where you ask them to do something, if interested, if ready to do it. The key is having enough people that you're communicating with at any one given time to generate the lead flow that you need to close a number of loans that you need to close in order to hit your goals.

That's another thing that many mortgage brokers overlook, GOALS. Any experts that you talk to are setting goals for themselves. What's your view on that as opposed to just being one of these standard loan officers who says, "I want to close as much as possible this month"? How important is having definitive goals?

It's imperative because you can't hit a goal you haven't identified; I don't want to get talking about this too much because we've heard it all a million times. Set your goals and write them down and then put mind triggers or whatever around you that constantly makes you think about that goal and track your progress. What I would focus on when we're talking about goals is obviously, number one, you have to decide what they're going to be and decide what you want to do in order to hit them; but more importantly, develop your game plan on how you're going to get there. Even a layer deeper than that, a part of that game plan is developing your system that's going to deliver that to people. Somebody might say, "Well, I want to close 10 loans in a month." In order to close 10 loans, how many leads are you going to need? In order to know that, you need to know things like conversion ratios, what your approximate dollar revenue per deal is, and have systems in place that produce consistent results.

When I employ loan officers, I can't just tell somebody, "Go out and close this many loans because that's how many you need to do," or if somebody's not producing well say, "You need to do more loans." That's an amorphous or abstract statement or comment; they have to have a step-by-step procedure or process that they do daily that leads to an outcome, that ultimately, will lead to their desired goal of closing 10 loans per month.

So, it's not just defining it; it's actually implementing it and being an implementer opposed to just someone talking about it.

Yes, when you're developing these different steps in the process, you design them so that they work together. If we talk about closing 10 loans, and in order to close 10 loans, you need so many leads, and you're going to make X number of dollars per lead, you also know how much money you're going to need for marketing. You'll track what you're doing daily, how many people you're talking to, and how many leads you have coming in. You'll have, essentially, a bad word I hate to use but it's essentially a budget on where you are at, at any given time. So, if you have determined you need 100 people to call you over the course of the month, that's roughly, if we're going to deal with working days per month, say there are 25 working days, you need to have four people calling you per day. If you get a week into the month, and you haven't talked to 25 people, you need to readjust or reevaluate either what your goals are or what your system is to reach those goals. It starts at the level of where you are obtaining the leads, the conditions under which those leads come into your office, what they're being told or presented, all the way through the process to when they become a closed loan.

How often do you think people should reassess their process and their goals to reach them? I guess to answer my own question, you put the action in place, then you go and reach that goal; but sometimes, people lose focus after 15 days, sometimes 30, some 90 days. They need to refocus and get that confidence of reaching their goals.

Right. You're going to do better if you have short-term and long-term goals. The more goals, the better; and really, you could call them goals, you could call them milestones, you could call them little tasks in between, and one task leads to another task, which leads to another task, breaking your process down into pieces. It makes it seem much simpler and easier to track than if you're just starting to go from well, okay here I am. I'm showing up on the first day of the month, and by the last day of the month, I have to have X number of units sold.

To receive your $247 in free bonuses: www.TheInsiderSecretsGift.com

We don't just pick up the phone, or people don't just call us and say hey, I want to buy a mortgage, and then that day we like made a mortgage sale. We have our money, and now we're moving on to the next one. There are a lot more pieces to the puzzle than that, so it takes some planning. You'll set short-term goals, mid-term goals, long-term goals; and I would say when you're first starting out, you're going to need to pay much more attention to those systems and processes than you will if you're running a system that's been going for five years.

I don't need to monitor things on a daily basis anymore. I can monitor them monthly because I have the track record and the history behind what's been proven to work, and it works consistently over a long period. I don't need to look at it daily, but when I'm developing a new system or process, say like a new marketing campaign, I'll monitor it day-by-day, if not hour-by-hour. I might monitor it lead-by-lead or deal-by-deal; I pay close attention because I'm doing something new. Before something is dialed in, before something is proven to work, I'm going to pay a whole lot more attention to it because I know it's going to need to work, or I believe it's going to need to work vs. a process I've had in place for an extended period of time and has already been proven to work. One core principle in what we specialize in doing with our borrowers in the actual mortgage business that I run is the automatic nature of what we do for them and how we get them out of debt.

When you're looking from a personal point of view in achieving goals, the more of the actions, tasks, and processes that you can put on autopilot or run automatically in the background without you having to do manual labor to make it happen, the more likely you are going to be able to stick with it. For example, if your system is, "I'm going to get out the white pages, and every day I'm going to call 200 people to try to generate a mortgage application or a group of mortgage applications," that process is going to be much more difficult for you to stick with over an extended period. However, if you say, "I have this display ad that I'm going to place in the newspaper, and I'm going to just have it run on Sunday all year," it's much easier. You can place that ad in the newspaper, and you pay a bill, and it runs every Sunday; it runs on autopilot. Take that a step further. You can put that ad in the paper and have it placed there on autopilot so that it shows up without you having to do work repeatedly, but you can set up a system so that when people call that ad, that's automated, too, so you're not touching it.

You start to build processes on top of each other that take you out of the day-to-day responsibility of having to work or run that system. It guarantees that it's going to be done over and over again. That's another example of leveraging your time, spending your time in places and areas where it has the highest dollar value to you. The last time I checked, the only time we are paid is when we have a loan close. I am not paid to generate a lead; I am not paid to convert a lead to an application or anything like that. I only am paid when a loan closes and I get a check from the lender of the title company. It stands to reason that the more time that a loan officer spends actually selling, getting a borrower interested in something, signing them up, making that sale, and getting that check, the more checks that they're going to get.

People will talk about getting referrals; and if you read what I promote, I'm not a big fan of getting referrals from third-party providers like realtors or CPAs or financial planners or whatever. One big draw is that they perceive those leads to be free, when really they are not free leads. People think, "I don't have to do marketing because I'm getting leads from this source." You really are doing marketing; you're just having to market to your lead sources. It's just a different type of lead source, so there is time and effort being spent there. Often loan officers spend so much time and energy trying to get a deal from, let's just use a realtor as an example because everybody knows and probably has tried to do that at one time or another, even me, which is why I know I don't want to do that anymore. You spend so much time and effort getting a lead that by the time you actually get the lead from the realtor, you're all worn out, and you don't even want to work it.

That comes down to picking your niche and your lead source.

That is right.

Thank you for your time today. It has been a great learning experience and I am sure that our readers will feel the same way.

Thanks, I appreciate it.

Chapter Three
Interview with
Chris Hurn

Chris Hurn is a National Expert in Commercial Lending. This is a very special opportunity to learn how to add an additional revenue stream to your mortgage career. Chris is the CEO, President, and Co-Founder of Mercantile Commercial Capital. He actively participates in, among other things, the business development, underwriting, and marketing functions of the firm. Chris specializes in helping business owners buy their own office space while increasing cash flow. This unique niche has catapulted Mercantile Commercial Lending into the Inc. 500 list of fastest growing companies in the nation. This is an amazing accomplishment for anyone to reach and Chris has done it. This interview will give you some insight that you will want to know, so you can capitalize on working with Chris.

How are you doing?

Oh, I have not ever been this busy, I think, since we've started the business. It is absolutely…we're just slammed. We're going to have our biggest month ever next month and we've got things lined up even bigger in October and November. It's going very well; I have to pinch myself and laugh at the fact that everywhere I turn in the media these days, the sky is falling.

Yes.

It may be in the residential world—I can't really speak from experience on that side a whole lot—but it certainly isn't from my world in the commercial space. Not at all.

It's amazing how the news only reports a little bit of what's truly going on. I get people who are constantly asking me, "Are you still in business?" Just because they heard the breaking news that mortgage lending is tightening up and, like you said, the sky is falling. Today, let's go ahead and get into what you do and how you position yourself to be so successful in the commercial sector. Let's start by talking about some of the differences between residential and commercial financing.

Personally, I don't do any residential whatsoever. I never have. I never will. The only thing I've ever done is commercial real estate financing in my business, my role, as a financier. There are a number of reasons for that. My perception, rightly or wrongly, is that residential is much more emotional. Commercial doesn't have that "I like purple curtains and, therefore, we're going to buy the house" situation. It's business people presumably making more logical choices, not as many emotional choices, so, to me, I think it actually knocks out a whole level of frustrations and problems. So, that's one reason I like it.

Having said that, the commercial market is very fragmented. Because the residential market is such a bigger market and there is so much more fluidity as far as deals and properties, properties don't sit on the market as long as they could in commercial. This recent situation is perhaps the exception. Because of that, my perception as an outsider is I've seen that the residential world has gotten much better at making a paperless office type of thing. That's been around for 20 years. That's a big goal. Well, residential has made a heck of a lot more headway in that than the commercial side has. I can only name one or two software programs out there that are even geared towards commercial lenders, but residential lenders have all sorts of things. I think that you can literally take an application over the phone and process something on the computer and if it hits certain boxes—boom—you can issue it to them on the spot. There are a lot more nuances on the commercial side and it's a mixture of art and science. It's not as scientific as the residential world, which has done a good job of that over the years. So, that's another piece. Candidly, that means there are more opportunities for me because I can play on that fragmentation, on those unexploited opportunities, on those spots in the marketplace where they're not getting the kind of attention that they really ought to. So, it works really well to my advantage.

There is also timing, of course, and I guess all this plays back to what I've just said which is, I talk to mortgage brokers all the time and we probably get 10 to 20 calls per day here *from noon*. Usually, they have a horrible, crappy deal that we don't want to touch, and we try to educate them a little bit. We try to educate them briefly on what we're looking for and then kick them off the phone and send them on their way and, hopefully, they'll bump into something that fits later on. But to think that we can close on a deal in four days just doesn't happen in the commercial world. Most of it's not because of anything on our end; it's just part of the process. We have an expression out here—we hurry up and wait a lot on people and third parties. A commercial appraisal, for instance, is usually somewhere between 50 and could be up to 100 pages long. It's much more comprehensive than a residential appraisal. We don't have the commercial equivalent of a "drive-by" that you have in the residential world. We really don't have people sitting there with their laptops who can pull up a value instantly. I don't think there's even anything online that can tell you what your commercial property is worth. So, these things take time. Unless you send a heck of a lot of deal flow to a commercial appraiser, it's going to take three, four, five weeks to turn around a commercial appraisal, in general. I've been known to get them done in a week to two weeks, but usually that's for the people we're sending a lot of volume and business.

Surveys take a long time on the commercial side too, especially if we have to redo them. We have an environmental report to consider on many commercial properties; that takes time. Usually, there is a deal-breaking attorney involved that is screwing up title, and we have to deal with that as well. There are many of these types of things that elongate the commercial process from start to finish, and I think that has given the commercial side a bad rap in many residential mortgage brokers' minds. It's unfortunate that they can't be a little more patient. A 45- to 60-day cycle is common in the commercial world and most commercial contracts with reputable commercial real estate agents and brokers will write them for 45 to 60 days to close. That's reasonable. Most competent lenders could hit those goals without any trouble. I think the fastest closing we've ever had is 27 days from the first phone call or e-mail until we were at the closing table signing docs. But 27 days, to a residential person, probably sounds like an eternity.

Those are some examples.

There are some different types of commercial financing in reference to different lenders specializing in different things. So, what kind of commercial loans do you do?

We focus only on financing commercial properties for business owners, and when I say business owners, I mean small and mid-sized business owners. We do not finance speculators. We never have and never will. That's part of why we're having this call on August 30, 2007, and you know, the sky is falling, if you listen to the media, about the residential world. We don't have those issues. Way too many people finance speculators, and that's not something that we've ever done nor will we. We're extremely targeted on our niche. We are the only commercial lender in the country that leads with what I think is the absolute best commercial loan product, and we'll talk about that later. Only when someone does not qualify or is not eligible for that product, do we ever roll out our "secondary things." We can actually do a conventional commercial mortgage like a bank would. We also can do commercial stated loans that most banks do not do, which no banks do actually, but we do and that market is still out there. We primarily lead with those three products. We do have an investor product that we don't really do much of. It's an occasional thing we'll look at and, often, you're still going to have the owner present; the borrower is still going to occupy a little bit of the square footage, maybe 10 percent or 15 percent or 20 percent of the square footage and the rest he'll lease out.

To receive your $247 in free bonuses: www.TheInsiderSecretsGift.com

Then we also have a multi-family product, but it's really going to be for properties with between 5 and 100 units. Anything below that is considered residential. Anything above 100 units and every lender falls all over themselves to try to get those deals. We won't even try to focus on this area. That's pretty much it. Because that is our focus and because we know our niche, we don't try to be all things to all people. We clearly know what we're going after. We don't have the economic vagaries that other lenders have.

A business owner, generally speaking, always wants to own their commercial property once they know they can do it in a smart fashion, and they don't have to cash out everything they've ever saved to put money down. Later, we'll talk about how we differentiate ourselves from most commercial banks in the commercial space. So, they all want to stop throwing away their money on rent. The only time they don't is when they think they have a company they're running that may go public someday and, obviously, Wall Street analysts will look at a ratio like return-on-assets and you don't want to have real estate on your balance sheets because it screws up your return-on-ratio. But, most of the time, because our focus is on small to mid-sized business owners and most of them realize because of the tech crash in the late-90s, their exit strategy is not an IPO. Their exit strategy is probably to sell their business some day or to gift it to their kids or simply to shut it down. So, if that's the case, then it makes no sense making your landlord wealthy at your expense. You may as well pay yourself the rent. Your business is going to have to have a facility to operate in anyway. You may as well pay yourself and build some equity by owning the commercial property. That's exactly the space that we focus on—a buyer who does not really deviate much with what happens in the economy.

Now, if we go through a depression, there are going to be people not wanting to buy commercial property, but we're not going to go into a depression. We may head into a little bit of a recession but I'm not even totally convinced that that's going to happen. So I think this is just a lot of hysteria over nothing right now because "when it bleeds, it leads" and the media is focused on that pain. That's what everybody is freaked out about. But, as I've said, we've never been busier.

Many small business owners feel that they can never own. They don't know how to go out and buy. So, what are some of the problems that small business owners encounter with conventional or ordinary financing?

The funny thing is I'm actually getting ready to do this. I'm trying to figure out the legalities of it, but it's like a mystery shopper. I'm going to do it like *Laugh In* or one of those types of shows, you know, where I actually have a secret camera on. I'm going to do that, film it, and then obviously black out the person's face and bank name and whatever, but I'm going to pretend to be a potential borrower and film what somebody actually goes through. I already know what happens, but I have to show that to people so it resonates even more with them.

But what would happen if you and I went into this, we'd sit down and we'd say we found a million-dollar office warehouse we want to buy. We've been in business five years, and we're tired of paying our money to rent and it's time that we want to buy this.

"What can we do with your bank?" Every business that's in business has a banking relationship. "What do we need to do, Mr. Banker?"

The loan officer will say, "Great, that's wonderful, let's go ahead and do it. We can do 75 percent or 80 percent loan-to-value."

Let's pretend we're manufacturers, "What exactly does that mean, Mr. Banker?"

"Well, that means, on your million-dollar purchase price, you're going to have to put down $200,000 to $250,000, so up to a quarter of a million dollars."

You say, "Wow, that's a lot, you know, between the two of us, we hardly have two pennies to rub together. We were thinking we might be able to do this with a little bit less, I mean, when we bought our homes, we got like 90 percent financing or 95 percent or 100 percent or whatever. Is there anything like that in the commercial world?"

The banker will hem and haw, there will be this big dramatic pause, and he'll say, "Well, we really don't have that. The only thing we have is, I guess, we could perhaps do a small business loan. You know, you've probably heard of the Small Business Administration? It's a pain in the butt, they make it really difficult, but we could probably do that and, because your deal is less than $2 million, we could certainly take a look at that."

You and I will go, "Great! Well, how much do we have to put down then?"

"Well, we could maybe do 90 percent loan-to-value, put $100,000 down."

"Okay. We can liquidate some of our savings and I think we'll be able to manage." So, he'll give us a big stack of stuff to get together for him and we'll run off and fill it all out.

Now, what hasn't been said is what's interesting and I hate to be like a conspiracy theorist but this is the God's honest truth of what happens out there. The banker only offered an SBA product secondarily. They did not lead with it. They already pooh-poohed the SBA, badmouthed it, because bankers don't like to deal with it. And, the SBA has been a pain in their ass over the years. They also only offered one SBA product. Most bankers will not offer an SBA product for loans larger than $2 million dollars. Now, the reason they do that is there's a well-known SBA product called a 7(a). It's had its ups and downs over the years. A few years ago, it was in the press all the time because Congress was wrangling over the SBA's budget.

The bottom line is, it is a floating rate loan for a business owner to buy commercial property, although they can also buy another business assets with it, do a business acquisition loan, get working capital, pay down their payables, buy inventory, start up capital, all sorts of different things. It has a whole host of proceeds, refinance, etc. The problem is, if you think about this from a smart investing standpoint, you don't buy a hard asset like commercial real estate with a variable instrument, with a prime-based floating rate, which is what it always is. It's always going to be the *Wall Street Journal* prime or U.S. prime rate, which, today, is at 8.25 percent plus the spread—that's how they come up with the interest rate. And so, as prime goes up, which it did, like 17 times or so about two years ago over a two-year stretch, all those guys with an SBA 7(a) loan get hurt and, of course, they wail and scream and gnash their teeth and that helps to give the SBA a bad reputation. But the problem started with the banker—that was the only loan they offered in the first place.

By contrast, we offer an SBA product that is in the shadows of the 7(a). It's about half the size in terms of annual volume of 7(a) product and not nearly as well known. It's a phenomenal product. I even have one myself; that's how much of a believer I am in it. Bankers are like you and me; they want something simple and easy. They don't want to have to work very hard. They'd rather go play 18 holes at the country club, and put their wingtips up on the desk, that type of thing. So, they first want to offer their own conventional deal because they could approve it in-house and all bankers are paid either a bonus or commission based on the loan size and the assets they're bringing in to the bank. If they do a 75 percent or 80 percent loan-to-value deal, that's pretty good. If they do a 90 percent SBA loan, that's not bad either because, obviously, it's a little bit bigger loan, but it's a little more hassle to them, But they'll do it sometimes.

The difference is the structure. You're going to find my loan is a much smaller loan amount for the bank and there's a reason behind that, which we'll get into in a few minutes. Therefore, they don't make as much money on these deals and that's one reason they don't promote the 504, which is what we specialize in. We've become the acknowledged nationwide experts at it. They don't promote it because they're making a lot less money, and it has a little bit more perceived hassle in their minds. It isn't to us, because we do them all day long, every day, but if you only do one or two of these a year, it's like brain surgery. So, that's what really happens.

The other issue underlying all of this is the phrase that "cash is king" for a business owner and it certainly is. But the bank always wants to lower their own risk, even at the expense of and increasing the risk of the small business owner. So, a bank is always going to want you to put as much cash down as possible in a deal. That's why their conventional deals are 20 to 25 percent down. If they do an SBA loan, they're actually getting a guarantee from the U.S. government from U.S. taxpayers on that loan, but they want to minimize their risk so they ask for more cash. The problem is, if you're a growing, healthy small business, you can't have all your cash tied up in an asset like commercial real estate, which is maybe only appreciating three to four percent historically a year. Yes, you're not paying somebody else your rent, but you can probably make a much better return from that equity savings if you didn't have to put quite as much cash down. That's what many people fail to recognize at first, and what we educate our borrowers about every single day.

Let's talk a little bit more on why small business owners are better off not going with their bankers' loans and instead working with someone like you who specializes in something that bankers view as a little tougher.

Well, there's an attitude issue. I'm an entrepreneur. I'm just like the borrowers I finance. Bankers have the stereotype of being conservative and buttoned down for a reason. Most entrepreneurs aren't that way. Bankers are more about protecting their banks than they are about helping a potential client and that's unfortunate, but that certainly is the case for most commercial bankers. Partly because of that, they have slower approvals. A slower approval, in and of itself, isn't necessarily bad. The problem is it creates more anxiety on the part of small business owners.

To receive your $247 in free bonuses: www.TheInsiderSecretsGift.com

I don't care what anybody says, you can have pristine credit. You could have an 800 or an 830 credit score. The bottom line is that anytime you go into a financing situation, there's that small inkling of fear in the far recesses of your brain that says, "What if something screws up, a technicality happens, and they don't approve me?" Everybody has that thought going on and the quicker you can extinguish that, the better it is. So, you work with a bank, you're going to have slower approvals, everything is going to take longer. I can't tell you how many deals we've had over the years where we'll issue a commitment literally weeks before any competitors get back to them. It's hysterical to us sometimes. So bankers don't understand their loans, and they have slower approvals.

Many times the terms on commercial loans from a bank are much shorter than what we would offer. Again, this goes back to the whole risk thing, as banks are risks adverse. They're always trying to mitigate their risks, trying to manage their risks down. The problem is by doing that, on a continuum, it increases the risk to the business owners. So a banker will do a 15- to 20-year amortization on a commercial property, which is extremely common. I would offer a 25-year amortization schedule at Mercantile. Right there, I've actually increased that business owner's cash flow because I've put it on a longer term. Now, that doesn't mean I'm trying to make more interest on them, but yes, he would pay more interest if he carried it the entire 25 years. Candidly, in business—this is another difference between residential and commercial—it's all about what can you do with that cash. What otherwise could you do with that cash? If you can actually have smaller monthly payments because you have a longer term on your loan, then that means you have more cash flow that you can actually deploy to grow your business even faster to make more profits. If the cost of the money right now to own commercial property is 7.5 percent and you can't make more than 7.5 percent by reinvesting that cash in your business, then you have a problem.

Most of the time, when business owners are educated enough and they understand this process by talking to somebody like us, they come away believing it's almost a fiduciary duty to put as little down as they can on the commercial property. They can do so much more and get much higher return on their investment somewhere else with that cash. Often they don't understand that and, if a banker doesn't talk about it, which most of them don't, the business owners, who have blinders on, are often too focused on whatever it is that they do. They see patients, they make widgets. The banker supposedly is the expert at commercial real estate financing, and what the banker says they usually go with. It's really unfortunate. I've seen so many people taken advantage of over the years because of this very thing.

Also, most bankers are generalists. We're not. We are absolutely specialists. We know more than any banker in the country about exactly what we focus on, and I would defy anyone to prove me otherwise. We've seen every scenario there is. It's another reason bankers try to shrink away from the financing that we do; they just don't have any expertise in it. As I said before, they only do one or two of these a year and it's really, really tough. They're much more focused on doing a conventional deal and then, "Oh, by the way, can I give you a line of credit? How about we look at your auto loan? What about your home loan? Can I move your deposits over here? You know, we just bought this little insurance company, how about we do some insurance for you?" and all this other bullshit...I get a little worked up about this.

The way I describe it is we offer five products. Five loan products, and we do them better than anybody. We're competing against most bankers who are offering 45 products and services. We don't do any other banking products or services other than the five commercial loan products that we offer, and so you have this situation where we're the experts. We're clearly the specialists; we're competing against generalists who are basically like the vendor in Times Square opening up and saying, "Do you like these watches or these watches? What do you want?" We don't have to do that. We're focused on the immediate need, which is the financing of their commercial property. I don't give a crap who he does his banking with. It doesn't matter to me at all. It's not what we're about.

We have the national and the local awards to prove it. The national awards are a testament that proves we are the acknowledged expert in what we do. I told you before, we use our own products, that's how big of a leader we are. You probably couldn't find a handful of commercial bankers in the entire country who believe in their own product enough to actually use it, nor are they entrepreneurial enough to actually see the value of owning your own place. They're not just a number with us. If I go to Bank of America and I'm a small businessperson, I'm just a number to him. Who cares? I would only contribute a half a percent of a half a percent of a half a percent of a penny to B of A's earnings. Well, if they come to us, it's a meaningful piece of what we do. We take care of that person. Again, I go back to our focus; because we're so focused, I don't care about all of the other banking products and services. We want to just deal with the immediate need, which is the financing of their commercial property.

Last but not least, the other reason to deal with somebody like us, is we're leading with the best product always. There's no sort of ulterior motive with us. Are we leaving some money on the table sometimes? We probably are, but our borrowers come back to us in two or three or four years with another property they want to do and they want us to finance it. There's no question who they want to work with. They refer all their friends to us. They tell many of their business associates about us. Therefore, we mostly deal in referrals these days. I mean, we only take inbound calls. We don't make any outbound calls unless we're doing what I call a "celebrity" voice blast, but generally speaking, it's inbound only and it's all referrals. It's tremendous. You can't do that if you don't actually perform well and truly focus on what matters. So, with us, most of our borrowers are putting half to a third of the money down on commercial property when they finance with us as compared to their bank. We almost never lose a deal. We compete against the banks on the commercial mortgage scene.

We also have longer terms, as I've said. We're doing 25 years, whereas most banks are doing 15 to 20 years. Those are the basic reasons it doesn't make sense to work with a bank in most cases.

Many residential people or even businesses have no clue about the process of commercial mortgages. They think it's a mysterious process, and it's difficult to go through. Can you walk me through the process from beginning to end?

To receive your $247 in free bonuses: www.TheInsiderSecretsGift.com

Let me comment on that real quick. See, it's this mythical process that, in the interest of commercial lenders, they don't want to deal with a bunch of residential guys. They don't want to reveal all the secrets. I laugh about it and say, "Look, I'm going to pull back the curtain and explain it all to you." We're rolling out a nationwide correspondent program where I train our guys. They sign up, and they have access to an exclusive program, so if I sell to a guy in Cincinnati, he's the only guy in Cincinnati we're going to work with until he screws something up, and we go re-market Cincinnati. The bottom line is, we teach them all they need to know about how commercial is different from residential, how we formulate debt service coverages, etc. It's really not that complicated.

But the brilliance of it all is being able to take something that, on the surface, looks complicated and simplify it and make it understandable. Those are the truly gifted people out there. The teachers who can explain stuff like that. The problem is that most people in the commercial world don't want to do that. They want to maintain that barrier. They want to maintain that wall that prevents all the residential guys from getting into their business, because obviously, it's in their interests not to have more competitors. They don't want to have to compete against all these residential guys. It's really a shame. From a positioning standpoint, it's great for us because we're the only people on the residential guys' side and say, "Look, it's not as hard as everybody's made it out to be over the years." You just have to work with the right lender. You have to work with somebody who actually knows what the hell they're talking about. You have to work with somebody who can simplify this stuff for you and make

To receive your $247 in free bonuses: www.TheInsiderSecretsGift.com

the processes simple for you to systematize everything, and here it is. So, that's what we do with our guys.

How does commercial financing actually function from beginning to end, so our readers have a better understanding of how they can get commercial deals done, especially when they have the ability to work with you?

Well, let me give you some of it. We don't have time to go over everything right here, and you don't have enough pages in your book for me to cover everything. The bottom line is we try to take away the anxiety associated with financing right away. One thing we do is what we call a "Pre-Approval Process." It's something I ripped off from residential years ago. Many sophisticated, successful residential guys will not work with a borrower unless they have a pre-approval or a pre-qualification letter from a lender. I think that's brilliant. We use the same thing over here. Not a lot of commercial lenders do that. I offer them a guaranteed 24 hours or less, 39-step pre-approval letter process, which is trademarked. The bottom line is, I get seven documents from them (I'll explain what those are in a second), and we go through a 39-step process, basically evaluating everything, which gives us about 90 percent of our quantitative underwriting of what we need on the deal. We go through all of that, and we spit out in less than 24 hours about a four-and-a-half to five-page pre-approval letter. This is not a term sheet. Usually, the term sheets that people give that are a page to a page-and-a-half from a bank aren't worth the paper they're written on. You know what to do with *that* paper.

This [Pre-Approval Letter] details all their financing, explains exactly what the terms are going to be, the estimate on the rate if we were to close today, the estimate on the monthly payment today, how much money is down, the collateral, when it expires, how much of a good faith deposit is required for us to proceed forward, etc. We also always include a checklist of additional documents we had to turn that pre-approval letter into a commitment letter. It's really simple. It takes about 20 minutes to do it, to go through those seven documents and get it over to us, including most of that is actually digging some things out of files.

You see, if you're an operating business right now, we do have some start-up fields, but it's rare. It's usually only going to be a franchise/turn-key type operation that we would finance. It would be like, say, if you were a franchise daycare center or franchise restaurant and you had to have real estate as part of your project, only then would we probably take a look at it. Most of the time, we're dealing with businesses that have been around for a little bit. It could be two to three years. It could be 20 to 30 years. So, they're all operating companies, it's not very difficult to dig out some of this stuff. The first thing we have to know is an estimate of the project costs, which they may not know, but often they have a good idea or if you have it under contract or have a letter of intent, we'll go off of that. We do some estimates based on closing costs, are they going to have some renovations or not, are they going to buy any furniture, fixtures, or equipment (FFE), different things like that. We'll take a look at all that. That's number one, we have to have a starting point.

Number two, the last six things of the seven, are perfectly symmetrical with each other. Three things on the personal side, three things on the corporate side or the operating company's side. The first thing is tax returns. I need to get three years personal tax returns, and I have to get three years of corporate tax returns, perfectly symmetrical. The second thing is I have to get financial statements—personal financial statements and they have my form in the application or they can use somebody else's. See, that's how idiotic some bankers are. If you don't put your personal financial statement on their personal financial statement form, they won't accept it, which I think is asinine. I don't have a problem with that, I don't care, but that's, again, back to us being reasonable, flexible, and entrepreneurial.

On the other side of the financial statement equation, we have to get a profit and loss statement, a P&L or an income statement and a balance sheet from the business owner. So, now we've covered five of the seven things.

The last thing relates to debt obligations. We get an authorization to release personal credit to look at the personal debts that the borrower has, because we have to do a personal debt analysis—it's similar to what you guys do on the residential side—to make sure they can cover and service all of those debts. On the corporate side, we have a form that's called a business debt schedule, and we get a listing of any debts the business has that are long-term liabilities, not short term, so it's going to be things like a vehicle lease or car loan. Do they have some heavy equipment that they rent? It's not going to include the postage meter machine and the Xerox copier. Do they have a line of credit that they tapped a little bit? We'll take a look at all that. Based on all of that, we sort through it, crunch a bunch of numbers and spit out a bunch of stuff, and then we produce the pre-approval letter. The funny thing is, we don't need 24 hours. Candidly, we've got it down to such a science, that we've automated it so much now, that if it's a good deal without too many hiccups, too many things requiring explanation, we probably could do it in—I'm probably risking here telling you this, we probably could do it in less than 20 minutes. The problem is, nobody would believe it if I did it in less than 20 minutes. So I actually have to spend a day sitting there and then, if we're pretty busy, there's no guarantee I can get to it immediately, but if I got to it immediately, the whole thing probably takes less than 20 minutes, because we've automated everything so much and we do this all the time, which is great.

That is the first step of the process. Once we issue that, we try to have a checklist of any additional items we need. Those are application type stuff, sign your name a bunch of times, that kind of thing, nothing major. We usually issue commitment letters that match our pre-approval letters anywhere from three to five days. Again, most banks haven't even gotten back to them by then for even the first call. Maybe they've made a couple of calls, that we've actually already gotten a commitment letter. Maybe the bank doesn't have a loan committee meeting for another two weeks. We run into that sometimes, which is pretty humorous. We like to get our good faith deposit check after issuance of the pre-approval. We know that we provide the best overall value. There's no reason for them to go anywhere else and shop anywhere else, there's just simply no reason. Not to mention, usually they've already visited their bank, and their bank has never mentioned the phenomenal option that we obviously always lead with, which is suggestive their bank actually committing a lie of omission. There's no point in going anywhere else. They came to the experts. They came to the people who can do the best overall deal for them. They don't need to go anywhere else.

To receive your $247 in free bonuses: www.TheInsiderSecretsGift.com

We then get a check that covers us for any third party reports, which can, obviously, get expensive. Then we give them a credit on the closing statements for that good faith deposit as we close their deal.

We always have simultaneous tracks moving. We order the commercial appraisal. We order the survey. We get the title company in. We get the environmental report, if we need it. All these things are moving on multiple tracks at the same time, all in the effort to get that deal closed as fast as we can because, again, back to what I said early on, this is the only way we make our money. If that deal doesn't close, I don't make any money on it, so we are truly, perfectly on the side of our borrowers and try to get that deal done as quickly as we possibly can. The reality is, we're probably the most motivated folks involved. We literally drive the train to the closing table. Most of our borrowers really appreciate that. We've had many tell us that if we hadn't done that, been as consistent with our follow up and stayed on top of things as much as we did, the deal would never have happened. They admit that all the time. That's a "value-add" that I didn't even calculate early on, but we always do it.

That's great. Now, let's get into a little bit more about the specialization you have, because obviously, if people want to get this done, they need to come to you, being that you are the expert in it. What are some of the advantages of SBA 504 financing?

The biggest one, as I said earlier on, is it is an SBA product. The way I explain it to people is, look, FHA is a government guaranteed product. VA loans are a government guaranteed product. Plenty of student loans have a government guarantee on them. The bottom line is the government is usually pretty terrible at delivering its phenomenal products and services.

To receive your $247 in free bonuses: www.TheInsiderSecretsGift.com

However, they have some phenomenal programs. If you can become the expert, as we have in our space at one of those programs, you have a huge leg up on everybody else, and people would be absolutely nuts not to take advantage of it. So, having said that, most people think the SBA is a four-letter word. The reality is it's not. It has reformed over the last 5 to 10 years. It's a different agency than it's ever been. The way to think about it is: it just *happens* to be an SBA loan, but this is the smartest financing that a business owner can do when they factor in all of the other variables.

The biggest advantage is the down payment. They're putting a third to half as much equity down on that deal than they would with an ordinary commercial bank loan. Often, it's even more than that because what I didn't tell you earlier is we loan-to-costs financing, not loan to value. So, I look at the entire project costs—the purchase price of the building or if it's a construction deal, we take the land plus the hard construction estimate, plus the soft construction costs (which could be permitting, architecture and engineering fees). If they're interested, we'll put in furniture, fixtures, and equipment; we'll put in closing costs. We put all of that together and of that number, whatever it is, then we do 90 percent financing of it in most cases. If it's a special use property, we would do 85 percent. If it's a true start-up and a special use, we would do 80 percent. Again, the comparison is that most of the time, banks are not going to deal with true start-ups. Banks hate special use property and usually require an extra 5 percent, 10 percent, maybe even 15 percent equity if it's a true special use property, like many restaurants. Banks hate restaurants because, for the most part, what are they going to do with it if they have to foreclose on it? Now, you have a big thing sitting there with a bunch of stainless steel restaurant equipment, what are you going to do with it? They don't have a clue.

So, the biggest thing is that we're financing things loan-to-cost vs. loan-to-value, which for the banker is always going to be the lesser of the appraised value or the purchase price. All the time people come in and say, "Well, look, I got a good deal. I have an appraisal that says it's worth a million, but I have a contract for $800,000, Can we finance it off the million?" No, I can't and you're not going to find a commercial banker who can. You want to go to a hard moneylender? Fine. Maybe they can do it. But no reputable, legitimate, commercial lenders are going to do that. It's a struggle, but most closing costs are going to be another 2 to 3 percent on top of it that they're paying out-of-pocket in addition to the 20 percent, 25 percent, 30 percent down that they have to pay. It adds up quickly and there's a huge difference between us and every other ordinary commercial bank we compete with. So, that's number one.

The number two thing is the terms. We've already talked about that. Most of the time I'm offering them 15- to 20-year terms—I'm talking about the amortization schedule here, of course—vs. doing a 25-year amortization. It makes a difference. It makes a difference in cash flow; that's why people like it. Again, you can prepay it early if you want, but it sure is handy to have a 25-year amortization schedule that you know you don't have to pay all that every single month if you don't want to. Because there are going to be times in a business owner's career with some ups and some downs and, in the down time, I think he'd rather be on a 25-year amortization schedule. So, that's the second one.

To receive your $247 in free bonuses: www.TheInsiderSecretsGift.com

Rates. Believe it or not, this goes back to the SBA 7(a) loan program. There's this fallacy out there that SBA loans are more expensive than ordinary commercial loans. The reality is the ones that we specialize in—the 504s—that's definitely not that case. Here is how we structure it:

Let's take a million dollar total project. We're going to finance 90 percent loan-to-costs, so a $900,000 loan amount. We come up with that figure, $100,000 of equity for the borrower, using a formula. We have a 50 percent first mortgage or first trust deed, if you're on the West Coast, of that total project costs, 50 percent, so $500,000 is going to be the first mortgage. A second mortgage is 40 percent; put them together, that's 90 percent, plus the 10 percent equity injection from the borrower in your million-dollar project. The 40 percent second mortgage piece has a government guarantee on it and is part of a bond issuance, and it is what's called a debenture. These bond exchanges happen every single month on Wall Street. JP Morgan Chase is currently the one who underwrites and issues them. They usually sell between $300 and $400 million a month to pension funds, college endowments and mutual funds. These have a second mortgage on commercial property. Because it has a government guarantee on it, the yield spread that the investors get on it is smaller. This spread has been greatly reduced because of the government guarantee, so they don't have to get as high of a yield on it, and the pricing actually is below market compared to what ordinary commercial banks put out there, and usually significantly below their pricing. Usually, it's a point to a point-and-a-half below what an ordinary bank is putting on the street right now, so that's 100 to 150 basis points. So, you have this factor on almost half

To receive your $247 in free bonuses: www.TheInsiderSecretsGift.com

of your loan. There is not cheaper money out there for a small business owner to buy commercial property. It simply does not exist. Larger public companies borrow money at much higher rates than these secured mortgage 504 bonds. Now we combine that with what we price the first mortgage at (being fairly competitive with banks), and what we sell at the balloon effective interest rate. That is, in fact, the interest that a business owner pays—the amount their accountant is going to report on their tax return—it's the blended effective interest rate that they're paying, from both loans.

Usually what happens, is we're either the cheapest guys out there on paper, or we're right in there with someone's bank and sometimes maybe we're 25 basis points higher, but it becomes difficult to compete with us when this is our specialized product. It's what we always lead with. We're the nationwide experts at it. When a business owner understands that we put a 7(a) loan from the SBA and a conventional commercial bank loan on the table, and our 504 loans, 9 times out of 10, the business owner is going to pick our 504 loan when they know about it. It's that clear cut. Just knowing about it, that's the key. Often they just don't know about it because, as I told you earlier, the bankers don't mention it; it's not in their interests to let someone know about it. So, that's a huge piece of the puzzle right there and, believe me, we don't sell rates, but that is one attribute that's an extra benefit you can throw in at the end and say, "Oh, by the way, go try and find cheaper financing on almost half of your loan. It isn't going to happen, buddy."

The last thing, which I've talked about earlier, is loan-to-cost. There's a big difference between us vs. the banks that we compete against.

To me, those are the four primary benefits of doing a 504 loan with us vs. doing an ordinary bank loan with anybody else.

So, how does this work with a business owner who already owns their property?

Well, that's the problem. Right now, the way the law has been written for this program, which has been around for 20 years, you can't do a true refinance on the property. That may change in the future. There's been lots of talk in the industry over the last couple of years for Congress to give us the go-ahead and open it up to do refinances as well. If that happens, the floodgates will open. The reality is, right now, we can only use this program to refinance property if the existing debt has been in place for less than nine months. Now, I know that may sound like it's a lot of gobbledygook, but here's where that comes into play:

A business owner goes to the bank, as we said early on, and the bank dupes them into doing a regular deal with 25 percent down. Say this business owner is constructing his building, and six months down the road, he hears about us and says, "Crap, wow! I put $250,000 down on my million-dollar construction project and once it COs [gets its certificate of occupancy], we're going to permanentize it and I was going to be at a 75 percent loan-to-value. I'd much rather only have to put 10 percent down, $100,000, is there any way I can do your deal and get $150,000 back?" And I say, "Yes there is, sir, because we're within nine months, so let's go ahead and get all of our ducks in a row, have it ready and waiting. As soon as we get that CO, we'll take out the bank's interim construction loan and go ahead and put in place our 504 loan." At closing, he'll get his $150,000 difference back.

Borrowers love that when it happens, and most of them don't realize this is even an option. Again, that's just one of many problems of opportunities if you're in my shoes.

When we have a commercial refinance, and we get them all the time, we just do it conventionally. I do those as well, or I'll do a commercial stated, if they need a little cash out, that's in our bag of tricks too. We can do that but you can't use a 504 loan to get cash-out unless it's within nine months and even then, it has to be for approved uses, not just cash to take to Vegas if you want.

With all the great knowledge that you just gave everyone, what does the ideal client look like for you?

Pretty much anybody who is a small business owner who has now made the wise decision that they want to control their destiny and own their commercial property. It's for healthy businesses. They have to have some profits. Usually, the best folks are those going from previously renting to now wanting to own. As I said earlier, we can do some start-ups, but most of the start-ups that we will do will have some sort of a turn-key business operation to it, like the Pizzeria Uno franchisee that has to have commercial property as part of it. We have done some spinouts, like, when you have a group practice of physicians and one guy's going off on his own after 10 years and wants to buy a medical office condo. No problem, we can do those, too. But it runs the gamut. We do franchise businesses. We do non-franchise businesses. We do many daycare and childcare facilities. We do hotels. We do assisted living facilities. We do tons and tons, obviously, of offices and office warehouses, industrial space for manufacturers and distributors. It's all over the board. We've done probably seven or eight dozen commercial condos in the last two or three years. That's becoming a bigger thing out there that I see all over the country. It hasn't made its way to every place in the country just yet, but land is a sparse commodity. God's not making anymore of it, and people are starting to realize. "Hey, I'm a four-person architectural firm, and I'm only going to be a four-person architectural firm. We're comfortable. We're happy. I only work three days a week, and I only need 1,500 square feet. It's tough to get a landlord to carve up a big space into 1,500 square feet, but I have this person down the street building an office condo project. Wow, that would be great." That's where they start. "I need to buy one unit at 1,500 square feet, design it myself so it fits my parameters, and oh, by the way, because they cater to business owners, entrepreneurs, it's only 10 minutes from my house, my affluent subdivision, as opposed to the 35-minute drive I normally have." It fires on all cylinders. It's great.

I don't do strip clubs, I don't do gambling joints, I don't do people who restrict patronage, so private clubs who don't like whoever, we wouldn't finance that person.

But generally speaking, most things. I actually saw a statistic years ago that said 98 percent of the businesses in America are eligible for the financing that we provide because so many of the businesses in America are small businesses. We don't do it for public companies. It has to be for profit. It can't be a not-for-profit, so as you can imagine, it's a wide spectrum.

Definitely. How would it work with an individual who owns a property through one LLC? Do they have to buy it directly through that company or are they able to split it up into another LLC that buys that property or is that considered a start-up?

No. No. It's not a start-up at all. We call that an eligible passive concern, EPC, and you can do it as an LLC. You can do it as an LP, a LLLP; there are all sorts of varieties. We actually encourage that to our borrowers and here is the rationale for why. We probably have 85 percent of our borrowers do that kind of structure. You really shouldn't buy the commercial property in your personal name, and you shouldn't buy it in your operating company name either. Someday, you're going to want to sell that operating company, but if you're wise enough to start with this in the beginning, to own the property in the LLC (and, by the way, the way you tie it together is with a 100 percent master lease that ties the operating company to the holding company). Someday you could sell the business and still maintain the property. For many business owners, that solves a huge problem they have. Most business owners, if they are honest with themselves, have not saved enough for retirement someday and this becomes a phenomenal asset that they have for retirement. They sell their business. They get a little income there, and then they sit back and cash checks from the commercial property because they've rented it out. Maybe they have the greatest tenants you could ever have; maybe they have their kids as tenants because they sold the business to the kids or maybe it's the new owners of their operating company—that's good too. Either way, you've got something of tremendous value now sitting there that you've been building up equity in it over the years. It's a great situation. So, yes, that's definitely eligible. We don't have any problems with that whatsoever. Believe it or not, there are bankers who don't even know that. Well, I could tell you tons and tons of issues that bankers don't know about this stuff, but that's one I sometimes hear. The bank goes, "No, we can't do that deal because we don't like that structure, you have to own it in your company name." Well, that's just idiotic.

Where is the best place for a broker or an individual to find out more information about you and your programs?

Our primary website is www.504experts.com. They can get a ton of information there, articles that I and other people have written. There are testimonials, awards listed that we've earned. So, they can go there as either an individual or a broker. If they are a mortgage broker who is interested in becoming one of our correspondents, I would tell them to go to www.ace-report.com, and they can get a whole bunch of information there about the opportunities we have. We have a unique business model, something that we haven't even talked about here, which makes for an extremely profitable situation for our correspondents should they be selected and if their area is still open. They'll get all the details there. And then, we have a whole bunch of niche web pages, I mean, I literally have like 5,000 keywords in Google and Yahoo! and all those other ones and I've niched all of them to appeal to the correct segments of our website and other web pages. So, for instance, if you type in "daycare finance," you're very likely to see one of our papers or ads come up, we'll also often come up in the top 10 organically, too.

We're still growing. Despite everything we've said here, I don't know that we've hit our full stride yet. We still have a lot of stuff we're working on, and improving upon, and the funny thing is, the residential stuff hasn't affected the commercial side one bit. While I used to compete on a deal with four or five other lenders, nowadays, it's down to one or two because many lenders had too much exposure on the residential side. Somehow, now they're turning off the spigot on the commercial side even though those things really don't have much in common with each other. So we're picking up more and more market share. It's times like this coming up when you can do that. When everybody else wants to shut down their market, that's usually when you should turn it up. That's the correct strategy that works most of the time. One of the greatest centurions is the third richest person in the world, Warren Buffet, and he's sniffing around many of these lenders these days, so I think there's a lesson to be learned there, too.

Anyway, that's how you can get a hold of me. If you want to e-mail me, you can e-mail me at info@mercantilecc.com and it will eventually work its way to me.

I usually only discuss this by phone appointment or e-mail, because I literally am slammed. I have 10 phone appointments today for instance. I have nine so far tomorrow. That gives you an idea of how busy I am. But we have tremendously competent folks here who work for me. I've trained them all. They all know my way of thinking. For most all of them, this is their first job out of college, so they didn't have any of the baggage most do in our industry, when they hop from bank to bank to bank.

That's another stupid thing people in my industry do; they try to hire bankers from other financial institutions and they bring all those horrible habits and baggage with them. I don't believe in doing that. I believe in starting from scratch, and I think that's the one reason we've just made it on the 500 list this year. We're the 245th fastest-growing, privately held company in America. We're proud of that, and it's something we just found out about a couple of weeks ago.

To receive your $247 in free bonuses: www.TheInsiderSecretsGift.com

Chapter Four
Interview with
Jessika Ondrick

Jessika Ondrick has created a very profitable career helping a unique niche of clients that almost every mortgage broker overlooks. She started her career in sales after dropping out of college and now owns her own Mortgage Company that is reaching numbers that are unbelievable to the average mortgage broker. Jessika tells you exactly how she has become so successful and how you can also by possessing a few qualities. She explains how having the WOW factor can take your career to the next level.

Jessika, you have such an intriguing story that I think it would be great to have you explain it our readers.

Absolutely. I decided that after graduating from high school, I would take a stab at college. While attending college I took a sales job where I called on small to mid-sized sporting good stores selling products such as Adidas, Gatorade and Starter clothing. These were easy sells due to the sporting good stores needing and wanting what I had to offer. When I got my taste of selling and the commissions that went along with selling, I knew that I would somehow, some way, become a saleswoman. Never in my wildest dreams did I think it would be in the mortgage industry. So, I dropped out of college after sowing my wild oats and minoring in "Having Fun," quit my sales job due to a jealous boyfriend who didn't like me being around flirty men all day and went to work as a nanny for Debbie Fields (Mrs. Fields cookies), which is a great job if you have a jealous boyfriend! I knew this was a dead-end job, but watching Mrs. Fields run her business and her family life gave me insight and firsthand experience of how to balance your life. Knowing that this was a dead-end job and that I would have to get a real job one day made it easy to keep my eyes open for new possibilities. I had a friend who was a teller for a small bank in my hometown and I had inquired about a similar position, and that's how I actually became a loan processor. At the time, I didn't even know what a mortgage was but fortunately, I was a quick learner, had great mentors and moved my way up through the ranks to Loan Originator Extraordinaire. I went from being a processor, making $1800 to $2200 a month to $15,000 my first month of full time commission/originating, and the rest is history.

That's a great story. It was one of those opportunities that you ran with and succeeded.

Exactly. I've had my failures along the way, but you have to fall down and skin your knees in order to learn. Not only will you learn, you will appreciate those sweet moments of success because you have unsuccessful moments to compare them to. I decided several years ago to welcome adversity, knowing that there would be invaluable lessons that would contribute to my success. This is true in business, marriage and motherhood. I've experienced many ups and downs in my career. The UP times are great and the down times make me stronger so next time I'm up, I'm up for a longer duration. Eventually I want to stay UP all the time!

Definitely. There are many ups and downs in the mortgage business, so what things have you done with your system to deal with the tougher times?

I learned early on that staying in front of your clients has to be the most important "leg" on your marketing stool. I believe in having a marketing stool that you constantly make stronger by evaluating, making necessary tweaks to each leg and whatever else is required to make it "earthquake proof."

I don't care if you have one client, you've done one loan, or if you have 10,000 people in your database, you have to stay in front of them. This is a simple idea that 98 percent of the loan officers out there don't do. It's important and crucial that you keep "connected" with both past and future clients.

When I say clients I'm not talking about just past clients, I'm talking about suspects, prospects and anyone else that you've encountered one way or another. It could be a realtor, a builder, referral sources, anybody that you would invite to your wedding, anyone that could potentially send you business.

Studies show that every month that goes by without connecting with your client, you lose 10 percent of your influence with them. Another crazy study shows, as mentioned before, that 98 percent of the mortgage professionals do not stay in front of their clients on a regular basis. They don't keep up-to-date databases. They don't offer value-added services. Yet they expect everyone they meet to remember who they are and what they do.

I watched my mother and father, who divorced when I was young, treat people both young and old, poor and rich, established and nomad, like equals. I loved watching people react to how they were being treated and I remember making a very conscious decision that I wanted to be "personable" and down-to-earth no matter what my life looked like. I wanted people to think of me and get a warm feeling so I have used that to my advantage in my mortgage business and I treat everyone like a "good ole boy" from my little country home town.

Staying in touch, keeping them informed and truly caring is the foundation of my mortgage business.

Because I have four kids, a husband, and several businesses, I have to make sure that I'm using my time wisely. So another one of my secrets includes an excellent assistant. I delegate as much as I can to her. I learned this the hard way because I'm a Type A control freak where I'm often quoted as saying, "I'm the only one that can do it right."

Yet at the same time, there were tasks that were slipping by and through the cracks that I wasn't getting done because I didn't have the time. For example, not returning a phone call. My excuse was well gosh, if I had returned all of my phone calls, I would have been calling people while they were in bed.

I started listening to myself make up these excuses and I thought, I am an idiot; people would rather hear from somebody than nobody. It doesn't necessarily have to be me; an extension of me is better than not calling at all. So after prodding and pulling from business coaches and people of that nature, I finally broke down and invested in what I call an "implementer," a.k.a., my assistant.

Now anything that I can't get to, whether it's returning an e-mail, returning a phone call, a campaign I've been working on for months and I just keep putting it on the back burner, I can throw to her and she'll get it done for me. At a certain level in your business, to go to the next level, you really have to have these types of systems in which you invest.

Your job has to be staying in front of your clients, and by having that contact with them, you're always going to be obviously top of mind. I've always said if I'm not staying in front of them, someone else is. I've seen a drop in business on months I don't send anything. There have been months in my career where I don't send anything. I mean there's actually been months, consecutive months that I haven't sent anything.

Then I look around going why am I not as busy as I was a couple of months ago? It's because I didn't send out my newsletters or have some form of communication with clients. Having an assistant helps to make sure this gets done as well.

Another thing that I would like to add is that by practicing the law of reciprocity, you are insuring your future pipeline. If you give, give, give; you get, get, get. Many loan officers close the loan and get their commissions.

It's amazing what happens when you start really investing in your clients. When I say investing, I'm not talking about spending thousands of dollars on them. I'm talking about

To receive your $247 in free bonuses: www.TheInsiderSecretsGift.com

time and pennies. It could be a phone call on their birthdays and wishing them a happy birthday or even singing a happy birthday song to them. As corny as it sounds, it's something I do and it's something that works!

Again, you'll hear me use that word "endear" a lot, but that's what it does—it endears them to you. They become raving fans. Now you have people knowing and thinking that you really care. You remembered. You remembered THEM! Sending balloons on their birthday is another thing I do. If they work in an office that has other people, sending balloons to them is interesting because now all of a sudden you're standing out and outshining anyone else's loan officer.

Again, it's that wow factor that I talk about, exceeding the expectations of your clients, and getting them to say wow, and just constantly wowing them. That's a part of my customer appreciation system that I really tweaked and tried for the last several years, and finally it's more systematic.

Before it was just like, oh, I haven't done anything for my clients in several months, I had better do something. Or hey, I had a great month, I should probably do something for some of my past clients. I had to get out of that mind frame because it was never systematic, and I just can't work without systems in place now. I'm not a robot by any stretch of the imagination, but I have to know that things are in order and working without me always being there.

It's just like a processor. If a processor is processing your file and they don't have a checklist to check off, or a way to keep the loan officer informed or a way for themselves to remember what needs done next, then how is that loan supposed to close and fund smoothly? I've had processors in the past that keep their processing checklist or parts of it in their heads. This is one of my biggest pet peeves and when I employ a processor or assistant, I am very clear about how our processes work. It's less stressful knowing that if we no longer employ any person that is a part of the process, that we are able to pick up a file and know EXACTLY what is going on in the file. We are also then able to replace this person easily. This is what I call a "Well Oiled Machine."

I often talk about "building an iron cage around your herd." This should be the case in every aspect of business. I constantly focus on building these "cages" around my employees and customers.

I like to use analogies whenever I can. Since I am a visual person, analogies paint clearer pictures. So let's paint. Imagine that you just met the person of your dreams, the one that you want to spend the rest of your life with. Now let's think about the process you must go through to either convince them that you are the one or verify that they are really the one. What does this process look like? I rarely hear of people getting married on the first date or first phone call…have you? Well to me, the process is similar when it comes to getting our clients to "marry" us. It's a process of dating and engaging. We have processes in our company that insure that our "dates" go well and that the engagement process is "cheat proof." I have a coveted checklist that goes through these steps and is always followed and filled out by my assistant. This checklist applies to suspects, prospects and clients.

One thing I really wanted to talk about is the successes that you have enjoyed in a male dominated industry. You talk about this wow factor; how does one go about possessing it? You're obviously a great source for knowledge on that.

To receive your $247 in free bonuses: www.TheInsiderSecretsGift.com

I have been told that I possess this "wow" factor. I had no idea what this really meant. I mentioned this before, it just really boils down to making sure that you're constantly under promising and over delivering. Nowadays you need to be constantly exceeding your customers' expectations. When you can figure out how to do this inexpensively and consistently, then you will get A LOT OF WOWS!

In my opinion, it's easy for a woman to possess it. By nature, women want to please and impress so with this combination, the wow factor can come quite easily. If it doesn't, it's easy to learn. Men, on the other hand, are usually "all business" but the men I know that possess this wow factor are more successful than their peers. Those guys who go about life as if no one matters but them will eventually "peak" and then crash and burn. I've seen this happen many times in my life and I can tell you that *they* don't possess the "wow" factor.

You always hear first impressions are so important. But you don't ever want it to stop there. You want to constantly be looking for ways to surprise the person you're working with and by making "things" happen.

I found that if you tell someone that you're going to get right back to them and you get right back to them that they are "WOWED" because so many people DON'T get back to them! I don't know about you, but I personally have heard countless times from borrowers that are shopping their loans, "I called four mortgage brokers and not one of them have called me back. You're the first one that ever called me back."

That blows my mind. It blows my mind today, but I was probably one of those mortgage brokers six or seven years ago. My schedule has always been somewhat gruesome so once I got better at delegating, the wow factor started becoming easier, not only to possess, but also to let shine through.

Anyway, so when I finally got rid of all these excuses and started delegating tasks, my life got better and my wow got bigger. Another thing that I do that contributes to the wow factor is I listen. I once heard a quote, and I actually have this on my computer at my office, and it says, "To be interesting, be interested." When I heard that, it hit me that the most interesting people I know are people that will take the time to listen to what I'm saying.

If someone walks into my office, they have typically been referred to me due to my expertise, which is helping borrowers who've had credit challenges such as bankruptcies, foreclosures or mortgage lates; some have possibly been enrolled in credit counseling. These types of borrowers most likely are a little embarrassed about what I'm going to see on their credit report or maybe the story behind what's happening in their life. So it's very important to have a big ear, and possibly even a hand to hold.

Now that non-conforming loans are harder to do, it's extremely important that you know the whole story. The whole story will get your loans approved. I can tell you that writing good explanation letters can get a loan approved vs. not caring enough to tell the underwriter a story. Especially on FHA loans, which I specialize in.

With the industry being in the state that it's in, the underwriters that are still around are taking their time to underwrite files. If there's something on the credit report, a gap of employment, or something along those lines, you really need to be able to explain it. Obviously, the only way to explain it is to know the whole story.

Women are born with "motherly instincts," which can really be to our advantage. I feel like that since I'm a good mother (mother of four) I'm able to listen to "both sides of the story," so by nature, I am a good listener. When you listen closely this will also help you avoid going back to your clients to get a question answered. This is the one thing that drives me crazy about people. A loan officer is like an attorney, and in order to win the case that you are representing, you must know the whole story so that the judge will approve it!

Fortunately, I have a lot of experience telling stories due to my processing background. But I find when my staff or I get lazy in our originating and processing skills it really shows in the approvals that we get or don't get. That is very uncommon but it does happen. So you have to listen, and when you listen the client will leave feeling like you cared, and that you have a heart, and hopefully they feel like you are different from what they expected.

With that, you hopefully wowed them. They're leaving your office going, "Wow—she really understood what we were trying to tell her, and hopefully she can help us." I talked to you a little bit about the customer appreciation program, and how I tailor my thank you programs for each of my closed loans.

Again, you're wowing these customers because you weren't just interested in them to make a buck. You really want to see them get back on their feet if they have credit problems. You really want to get their scores up so that they can get lower interest rates. You really want to see them get out of that non-conforming loan in a couple of years so that they can get into a lower rate loan. I think if you take that kind of approach in the mortgage world, you'll be around for the long run. I don't know about you, but I know many people who got into this business for one reason and one reason only, and it was to make a quick buck. Those people do not last. I'm watching it happen right now. It's estimated that HALF of the originators that were in the business in the beginning of 2007 will be gone by the end of this year. That's astounding and a much-needed process in our industry.

Ninety percent of my business is repeat clients and referrals. I'm not boasting, or bragging, or trying to pat myself on my back, but...

That's an ideal situation for any successful mortgage broker.

It's ideal, and it's so achievable if you'll just take the time to "map out your plan." Whenever I'm doing something, whether it's a marketing campaign or a customer appreciation program, I map it out. I know what I am trying to accomplish with the campaign and how it's going to unfold. I usually try to touch my clients (this is my database of past clients) at least twice a month. They obviously get my newsletter, and then I always want to send one more thing in the mail. It's something that would be a part of a campaign such as a book, a birthday gift, a "special invitation," a coupon, etc.

So if you're getting in the business for the first time, or you've been in the business for a year, or you've been in the business for 20 years, if you don't have a map then how will you know where you are going or how you will get there? This is like a goal sheet, but you truly mapped it out. How much money do you want to make this year? How are you going to go about doing it? I think you should focus on maps for campaigns and goal sheets several times a month.

That's great. What do you think the differences are between men and women in this business?

Well, that's a good question. As you're well aware, women are different from men in so many ways. These differences in life can make us very successful. I'm not talking about the physical differences, which yes, contributes to our success. A bat of an eye, a high skirt, or a low-cut blouse. I'm not talking about those advantages although those tactics do work.

I think women loan officers by nature care just a little bit more about the customer. When I say care, I think they just listen more. They maybe come across as if they care a little bit more. You hear many female loan officers complain about how much time they put into files. This becomes a double-edged sword; if you take the time to listen and really understand your customer and what they are wanting, they will rarely shop (at least in my experience). So taking the "longer application" can actually make you more money but then there is the flipside where you really want people to respect your time, so you have to be careful in this department. Work it…but not at the expense of your family or other areas of your life that might suffer due to lack of time management.

I often ask the women that work for me and the women that I coach, "What are some of the biggest regrets that you've had in your business?" Nine times out of 10 they'll say, "It's really about how much time I spend with clients" or "I don't stay in front of them like I should." We've already addressed how to stay in front of them, that's an easy answer.

In my opinion, you can never change a woman and her caring nature. You might take two-hour applications because you have the gift of gab. Or if you're a mother and you've got young adults in your office who remind you of your own kids and they're first-time home buyers, you're probably going to give them a little bit of motherly advice, and treat them as if they were your own children.

I've even heard of women watching the young kids while their client closes on the loan documents. I have a female loan officer that works for me who actually helps her clients move into their homes. It's just something that she does. I've asked her why she takes the time away from her family at night or on a weekend to go and move some of her clients. She said, if you look at the loans that she does, most of them are referrals, and it's because she really holds their hands and goes that extra mile. I think women don't think about going the extra mile…they just do it. In my experience, most men have to think about it.

I think going the extra mile can pay huge dividends. Now I'm not saying go and clean their house or watch their kids on the weekends or anything like that. It really boils down to a few things. You have to know what your time is worth. If you just closed a loan for somebody that made you $10,000, and it took you a couple of hours to take an application, and then your processor did the rest, going and helping your client move for three or four hours is really worth your time.

What happens is this, you spend more time with these people, but what you're actually doing is creating a client for life. So again I think it boils down to caring and going that extra mile. Women just have a way of endearing their customers. Again, if you're practicing the wow factor, then you're going to succeed.

You have to know your boundaries, of course, and not let people take advantage of you and your time. There's a fine line there I guess. Because we're born with these motherly instincts, we can really have those instincts work in our favor.

How does being a part of coaching programs and having your own coaching program for loan officers helped you?

That's where I took a turn for the better. It boils down to one thing: you're hanging out with like-minded people. You heard this when you were a kid, birds of a feather flock together, that is absolutely true. If you're flying with the right birds, you're going to go far. So that's why it's important to be selective with whom you're taking advice from.

Of course, I was coached and taught by the Guru Brian Sacks. That was the first step, and it was the right step in the right direction. When Brian formed his platinum group, I was the first female in the group, probably the first one to sign up because I knew that I needed to change something in my life. I was working way too many hours. I was doing way too many loans. My priorities were screwed up and I really didn't know what my time was worth.

When I started learning how to do fewer loans and still make the same amount of money or more, it changed the way I do my business. I decided what I wanted my life to look like and then developed my business around it. What

To receive your $247 in free bonuses: www.TheInsiderSecretsGift.com

a concept! This is how the most successful people in the world practice and live!

My life looked like this. Work 30 hours a week or less. I love to work and I love being self-sufficient. Spend a lot more time with my children and my husband. Take four more weeks of vacation each year and the list goes on. When I figured out how much money I wanted to make and how many hours I was willing to work to make that amount of money, my hourly rate became apparent. Now I had my "number." I also realized that I had some pretty bad time vampires in my life and it became clear that in order to reach these numbers and goals, I HAD to get rid of the vampires so this was the first thing I did! The rest is true history. My life has changed. I make changes immediately now rather than complaining about problems and hoping they will take care of themselves. I also read Dan Kennedy's *Time Management for Entrepreneurs* and I truly practice what he preaches.

Great book.

Great book. Oh my gosh, I read it from front to back (twice) on the flight back to Boise after being at my first mastermind coaching meeting. It was the first book I read from front to back in years. I was always just reading little bits and pieces of all these different kinds of books, but this one just grabbed me, and I resonated with it. I knew I had to make big changes right now, and the word implement came to mind.

I thought, you know what, I am not the best implementer but I'm going to start being one now. The first thing I'm going to do is to go back, and I'm going to implement exactly what Brian told me. For two reasons: first, I want to change my life and I know what my hour is worth now. Second, I have to come back to this coaching group in four months and if I don't make these changes, they're going to kick me out.

So there was added pressure.

I came back and fired three loan officers that I loved dearly. I thought I could just change their lives by teaching them all that I knew. But they were costing me a lot of money and a lot of time with my family. So I got rid of them, and a few weeks later, we had a couple of non-producing loan officers quit. I really started becoming this person that they didn't know. I was tired of being the cheerleader to losing players. I said, you know what, I'm not making enough money to help all these other people. The problem was that I believed in them more than they believed in themselves. I decided to focus on me and my family. As selfish as it sounds, I'm not going to become financially secure, have the financial freedom that I desire and want and deserve, if I keep worrying about everybody else.

This is why I have the best of both worlds now. I love helping people. I love coaching. Now I finally am paid for it. But I still get to run a mortgage business and work on my personal production. It's taken me a couple of years to get here and I'm still evolving.

Having a coach or belonging to a mastermind group can really help catapult your business. So either you want the change badly enough that you're willing to make a change that a coach suggests or you stay in the drudgery.

You told me that one of your favorite quotes is "The illiterate of the 21st century will not be those who cannot read, but those who cannot learn, unlearn, and relearn." What do loan officers need to be doing differently to keep a leg up on the competition?

It goes back to educating, becoming educated, and becoming coachable. I'm sure you have heard the saying, old habits die hard. It's one of those things where yes, they die hard, but you have to be willing to break that habit. I'm sure there are many examples of bad habits that loan officers have a hard time getting rid of but I think that there are many stubborn loan officers and spoiled loan officers in our industry. They think that because they have made a lot of money that they know everything. I've seen too many of these types of people crash and burn. To stay cutting edge, you must be educating yourself by attending seminars, investing in books and systems. We make it a point to bring in Account Executives from our list of approved lenders to discuss the latest greatest programs, marketing ideas, etc. Our loan officers love the fact that we are always growing with the industry and not staying stagnant. As soon as you think you know it all or aren't willing to keep growing, you die just like an un-watered vine.

Unfortunately there are still people who think like that.

Absolutely, and those people are just missing out on such unbelievable opportunities. I really think that the illiterate of the 21st century will not be those who cannot read and write, but those who cannot unlearn and relearn. It really says it all. I mean if you're not willing to learn new things, unlearn bad things, or relearn what you've already been taught, then you unfortunately will be the illiterate of the 21st century. That's the bottom line.

Education is key. I didn't graduate from college but I have always made it a point to keep learning. This is another reason I like mastermind groups. I get to learn from other loan officers in other states and who have different niches. It's a bonus if they have the same niche! You should be educating yourself at every stage in your life. Whether you're just graduating from college or you have one foot in the grave.

I shouldn't put it like that, but you know what I mean. You should constantly be learning new things. That's why some people really fail in being coached—they think they know it all. A gentleman came to one of our seminars. I'll never forget this guy.

At the seminar we have guarantees, if you're not a 100 percent satisfied with what you're going to learn we'll give you all your money back, we'll pay for your airfare, we'll give you a hundred bucks for wasting your time, those kinds of guarantees, and I'll never forget watching this guy. He had brought a few people from his office. They went over to explain to our assistant that what they just listened to was a waste of their time and they wanted their money back.

I was glaring at these people. I couldn't understand how they just sat in there for three hours and didn't learn one thing. I was a part of the seminar and already had four pages of notes! Long story short, we told the guy that he should have gotten a million-dollar idea in the first session and that we were sure that he would walk away with many million-dollar ideas if he would just stay for the remaining two days. He said that he didn't want to waste anymore of his time or anymore of our money (since we were giving his money back and paying for everything) but we insisted on him staying and us paying for EVERYTHING. Not only did this happen but the guy stood up at the end of the seminar and cried while he told the audience how embarrassed and ashamed he was. He continued to tell a sad story of him being a 25-year veteran to the mortgage business, how he didn't get to see his daughters grow up or his wife mature due to his long hours at the office. He didn't know that with some education that you could really build your business around your life. He didn't know that you could specialize in a niche and become an expert whereby you could charge more for your expertise. This man was going to be the "statistic." I'm happy to report that he invested in a few systems and is on his way to being a happier man!

He was well on his way to being insane. You've heard that saying, "Insanity is doing things over and over again and expecting different results."

That's a great story. There are always people out there that are going to think they know everything. Personally, I believe if you think you know everything in the mortgage industry, you might as well find a new job.

You have to be willing to learn in this business. Otherwise, you're right; you're in the wrong business.

If you had some last points of advice for our readers, what would that be?

I think it's important to make sure that you set your stage for success. What does it look like? If you were going to write a script about what your life looked like, how would it start, how does it unfold and what does the ending look like? You can have what you want if you are willing to work for it but dreaming about it won't get you there. You have to take laser-focused action! Be willing to learn and give back. Give back to the community, to your industry and to yourself! I also want to re-iterate to make sure that you only listen to people that you want to be like. Only take advice from those that make more money than you do and don't be a know–it–all. Accept change, keep inventing yourself, love what you do and IMPLEMENT!

Chapter Five
Interview with Tracy Tolleson

Tracy Tolleson has done the unthinkable as a Mortgage Broker. He has developed a process that gets Realtors to raise their hands and say, "Yes, I want you to be my mortgage broker." Tracy has over 183 Realtors that send him business and, more importantly, work on his terms. He works 30-35 hours a week, turns his cell phone off at night, and leaves the office Friday afternoon for the rest of the weekend. Tracy does all of this while making a high six-figure income.

Because he's done so much, I'll let Tracy give us a detailed background of his experience and knowledge.

Thanks. Well, I'm 46 years old, I live in Scottsdale, Arizona and I've been married to my lovely wife Vicky for 25 years this year. I've been kissing her on the lips, as I tell people—she hates when I do that—for 31. We have two wonderful children, two bad dogs and a brand new grandbaby.

We have done an awful lot in our years of being together, and at our age. So I know what it means to be committed.

My background includes dropping out of high school in the 11th grade and selling on commission from that time forward to this present day. I never punched a time clock. I have always sold for commissions or for business generation.

In the '80s, I was involved selling a $4,500 training course that had 350 hours of video and audio tape and weighed 72 pounds when it was delivered to your door. I successfully sold hundreds of them in less than two years via telephone, TV infomercials, conference calls and live seminars.

In the '80s, you had to have an operator hook 300 people up to a call at a time, and we would sell them via teleseminars. I sold through a 30-minute television show that ran on a local ABC affiliate in Hawaii. I sold a lead generation system that would attract them to the main product, and I have sold it from the stage in front of thousands of people.

Then I moved into the mortgage industry in 1991. So for 16 years I've been in the mortgage business. I started my career and weaned myself on doing hard money loans, 18 percent interest, 10 points, that was the deal, and I was very good at that. I was taught how, which is a key for your readers, taught how to package a loan, and that is a fundamental piece that has made me as highly successful as I am today because all the marketing you do in the world is great, but unless you can close the deal in the end, it doesn't matter.

I moved into residential purchases and refinances in the '90s, caught that wave. Then, after leaving a successful business and six-figure income in Florida, I moved to Arizona in 1996. I didn't know a single person in Arizona except for my friend Dan Kennedy and his wife. I started my mortgage business with a conscious target of working with realtors.

That was my preferred method. That was my only method. I choose to work with realtors in a format and fashion that would build my base of business on a foundation no matter what was happening with refis or anything else.

In 1999, I created a business system that attracted realtors to me, a system that got them to raise their hands and take a step towards me and actually opt-in, if you will, and check a box that said, "Yes, I want to be in your club. Call me up. Let's schedule an appointment and do business."

To give you an example, just this past week—in seven days through my marketing and business system—I had 22 realtors that I had never met, never heard from, never knew anything about, actually join my club. In a seven-day period, these realtors raised their hands and asked to meet with me, and I've already met with four of them. At the time of this writing and doing this interview, I have eight more scheduled coming to my office.

Today, I do coaching and consulting to the mortgage industry about my business system of attracting and retaining realtor referrals.

All through the refi boom of the early 2000 era, of course, I did refis, and 97 percent of my business from that point in 1999 to the present is done through referrals. I do no outside marketing to the public. I do not do any consumer direct marketing to the public.

Now, readers are saying to themselves, "Crap, I don't want to work with realtors." We know the story about realtors—disloyal, unappreciative, some people call them bad names just like they call us bad names. Why on God's earth would I want to work with a real estate agent or a realtor?

I've made all that pain and all that agony disappear to the point where your relationship now is established as professional to professional; you don't have to beg them for business. You don't have to take out rate sheets and donuts.

As we know, cold call selling sucks. That's the number one reason I see that people choose not to work with realtors—realtors or real estate agents. Before we created this, there was no complete system that encompassed all the points needed. To this day, this is the only one that encompasses everything you need to do to build that relationship.

So that's where I'm at now in my business and my career. I run a mortgage business myself, my own pinnacle club group chapter of realtors; there are 183 in my club right now, and I show people how to turn the realtor relationship into an oil well for your business. It's all about systems.

Without a system, any business is going to be far, far behind and likely not even to make it. A business that does have systems in place will succeed.

You are doing so much more than just running a business, which can be full-time task in itself. What is your key to doing all of these things?

It can be. I mean, running a business on its own, and we definitely believe in showing people that the key, the real secret of running a business—mortgage business, real estate business, anything—is having the systems in place that free you up and give you what it is you do best at and that is and should be selling and marketing.

In other words, it's about working on your business instead of in your business. Many folks have complaints in the mortgage business. This is typically how it works and then we'll get into how the realtors perceive things, so we can give the readers something real they can go out and do today.

Here's how it works. As a mortgage individual, you somehow stir up some business. As the book is being printed, most people are waking up every morning with this big gigantic fear, "Wait, where's my next deal coming from?" They're wondering what they have to do to bring in business.

So, if they happen to whip up some business, then it's very easy and the trap we fall into is we spend all of our energy and time micro-managing, overseeing, looking at these few business deals we've got instead of keeping our eyes focused on creating more.

I discovered a long time ago working with realtors, they're just like me. They're just like any business. Every day, they wake up wondering where their next prospect or lead is going to come from. Every day they have to fight the wolves off. Most mortgage people don't realize it, but every day, somebody else is waking up with the same problem trying to figure out how to steal your customer.

One of the best analogies in the world is a Loony Toons classic cartoon with Ralph and Sam. Ralph was the sheepdog, and Sam was the coyote. They were buddies and they'd go to the tree and clock in and then they became enemies, and every day it was Sam's job to steal the sheep in the herd, and every show was based on how he snuck around trying to do that. Every day the sheepdog had to keep him from doing it.

Most people don't want to work with realtors because they don't understand them in the first place, and then they don't have a way to actually put a system in place to attract them instead of pursuing them. Then, they don't understand the concept of a herd, building a herd. The mortgage business is fantastic. You can actually build two herds in the mortgage business—one, your clients; two, realtor referrals, and if you build a herd of realtors and that herd is trained, it becomes an oil well field.

There's a difference between an oil can and an oil well. An oil can is something you did a transaction with one time and it's useful when it's over. An oil well pumps it every day, every week, every month, and every year.

So, you learn how to build a herd of realtors, and you're not necessarily looking for the top producing realtor, more of the mid-level realtor, because they always stumble into several deals a year. Look at them as an oil well, what is an oil well worth to your business? If you have a herd of just 20 realtors and those realtors give you an average of three transactions a year for purchases, that's a very valuable herd.

That's 60 purchase units, and out of 60 purchase units, if the average fee is $4,000, that's a quarter of a million dollars—year in, year out—that you're going to receive if you don't do anything else, but don't screw it up.

You can have 183 realtors in your group, and one thing I know Dan Kennedy talks about is putting a fence or a cage around your herd. How do you develop the relationships to make sure you keep them long-term?

Well, that's a very good question. Part is the system that we've built and I tell everybody, Dan Kennedy is a co-creator of my business system. He put some polishing touches on it if you will, but we created and have The Pinnacle Club for Realtors, and this is what they become a member of.

When they join this, it is totally opt-in, they receive a host of benefits. They receive a monthly newsletter. They receive CD interviews, monthly coaching, and weekly sales tips. They are now part of a local group, and we now have chapters across America and growing every month.

So, putting the fence around them, as you say, is critical, and that is done by using what I call today's modern tools and equipment. Earlier when I mentioned that we were selling $4,500 training courses by telephone, we didn't even have a fax machine. Internet? Nobody had even heard of it. Computers were just coming out.

There was much more manual labor in those days in any business than there is today. We put today's modern-day tools and equipment such as call capture, direct response mechanisms, voice broadcasting, all those things that the reader may or may not have heard of that are part of successfully building a system.

In my case, I am touching my herd at least a hundred times a year. People will freak out over that. One key part in having a well-balanced mortgage business and working a successful mortgage business is you have to be balanced. I am amazed as a consultant to the industry how many people went through the refi boom, and I asked them how many people are in their database. Most can't tell me because they don't have a database, and then if they can tell me how many names are in their database, they aren't mailing to them. So, there's another valuable herd we can talk about.

But, I personally touch my herd of realtors in some form or fashion nearly a hundred times a year, if not more.

I imagine that gets expensive.

To receive your $247 in free bonuses: www.TheInsiderSecretsGift.com

With modern-day tools and equipment, I can give you those numbers, and it's very easy. Let's say it takes me five dollars a month to touch them. So, five dollars times 180 real quick, that's $900 a month.

Remember, I have a big club, okay, this is not standard. The reason I have a big club is that I've been doing it since 1999, but watch my own numbers. So, $900 a month to stay in touch with them, that's times 12. That's $10,800 per year, and I have only two out of all 180 give me one deal each. That's two loans. My average revenue on two loans is $5,000. There's my entire marketing budget for that year.

See, most people do not know their numbers in this business. It's costing me $10,800 and if I'm not good enough to get two deals out of that many realtors that have come to me and raised their hand, then you need to take me out back and shoot me. That's just the fact.

The title of your book states the concept, the reason the reader is reading this book is because they want to know the secrets. If you took and lined up a thousand of us—loan officers, lenders, mortgage brokers or whatever we choose to call ourselves, those that are lending money for a living—less than 20 percent are going to be able to tell their numbers of how any marketing or advertising works, and how you have to position yourself as the expert.

It's all about positioning. So, what we just talked about, that little scenario I gave you. You're right, the first reaction to everybody is, "Golly, that's going to cost me a lot of money." I would say to you, "No, it costs you a lot of money if you don't do that."

That's true. When things tighten up, most companies want to cut their marketing, because they have no way of tracking it to find out what is working and what isn't working.

Right. The reader is going to have two questions. So, back to the working with realtors, why should I do that? Ninety-eight percent of all loans in America, 98 percent of all purchase transactions, are financed. Out of that 98 percent, according to the National Association of Realtors, in something like 91 percent there are two realtors involved. Out of that 91 percent, there's almost 80-something percent that recommend somebody to do their loans.

That's a huge market! But I hear, "I don't want to work with realtors because I hate them." The second thing is, "I can't get the realtors because they're already working with somebody else." The third thing is, "I just hate them." Not a good mindset to have.

You leave a huge marketplace out there, but just like you said, it is all about looking at your numbers and understanding your return on investment. Again, if we go back to the oil well concept, if I do nothing but be consistent at spending my $10,800 on my herd and increase the number of referrals by only two each year, I've doubled my money.

If nothing changes, I've doubled my money because I pretty much pay for my marketing expense for the whole year off two loans, paid it again, pay it again. All I have to do is close an additional six loans in a three-year period and I've doubled my money!

I get excited talking about this, obviously. Let's go back to the herd concept. There are two herds a mortgage person can have. They can have their client herd, they can have a

To receive your $247 in free bonuses: www.TheInsiderSecretsGift.com

realtor herd, and I guess you can consider three herds, affiliates. Everybody's thought I'll work with CPAs. I'll work with financial planners, work with this, and work with that.

The point is herds. One reason I love the mortgage business is there aren't that many places with the option of developing different herds for different functions of your business.

How does your coaching program work to help these people to stay focused and attract, develop, and turn realtors into these oil wells that you're describing?

Well, they can find out more about it. We'll let them know where they can find out how the whole system works, but for example, as a reader of this book, you need to create lead generation marketing.

As you know, lead generation marketing attracts vs. pursues. It's a huge concept; when the reader understands it fully, owns it, and gets it, their whole life will change.

My system teaches and has built-in, already-created lead-generation attraction systems for the realtor. The realtor then comes to you. The realtor opts-in. The realtor tells you, "I like what you just told me. I want in. Please call me."

Then, my system teaches you how to handle that realtor in your initial meeting and develop that relationship. Then, you'll have a percentage of realtors that will understand and get it, and be looking to you for the professionalism they're hoping to find every day in their life.

I have something you can put in the book. It belongs to Vicky Tolleson. Ask yourself and ask realtors…Aren't you sick and tired of doing your own customer service for your own customer service? This is huge.

Put another way, aren't you sick and tired of having trouble spending your own money to get what it is you're spending your money on without having to do it yourself? Everywhere you turn, you have to do your own customer service.

I can promise and guarantee you that you can ask realtors and they are looking for somebody that will deliver. Then, you don't have to beg the realtor for business, since you have positioned yourself as the expert. My system teaches you how to position yourself as the expert, the expert at working purchase transactions, the expert at being the choice above and beyond all other choices; it shows why they should be doing business with you.

Then, it compels them to hand you their deals on a silver platter and trains them. My whole system is how you make $100,000 and more working 30 to 35 hours a week, no weekends and two months off in the year. I have lived that for the past 11 years.

This should be appealing to all mortgage brokers who are working 10- to 12-hour days. They're spinning their wheels and chasing business as opposed to having business come to them.

That's correct.

Many people got into this business to make a quick buck. They knew they could make good money, but they didn't know how they could sustain that money if the market tightened up. Your system obviously allows them to stay consistent in all markets, make money and have a life.

Exactly, and the past four or five years in the mortgage business and the real estate business was like a giant raging river; any idiot could stick his bucket in and come up full. Same for realtors.

Now, that river is not raging, and only those who know how to work, know how to apply, know how to have and get systems in place, will be able to take full buckets out of the smaller river.

I really don't complain or worry about what market I'm in because it's not going to change for me. It only gets better.

Once you can take that fear, anxiety, and worry out of your life, then you're on your way. It doesn't matter to me what's happening in the subprime world, what's happening with the interest rates, what's happening to this or what's happening to that. I know all the horror stories and objections.

You never have to worry about where your next deal is coming from. You can always be free of anxiety. You can lock in a steady predictable stream of income that you set for yourself. You can stop prospecting. You can stop normal advertising. You can regain control of your time and life, and you can be the envy of every other mortgage broker, lender or whatever in your immediate area.

You really can. Here's an interesting story for your book. I have a client in Honolulu, and he actually has the largest real estate company in Hawaii paying him every month to come to their meetings and teach their realtors basic mortgages 101.

Then, he gets to tell them about the local herd they should be a part of, and they pay him. You name another mortgage person in this country who's being paid by a real estate company to come teach their people and then tell them to go and give this person your business. I'll buy you the biggest steak in the country.

This defies how people are trained in the mortgage business.

Yes, it defies all the rules. It defies everything. People have a hard time believing that. No, you really got somebody that's taking your system, and there's a real estate company paying him? Yep, every month, in fact, at the time of this interview, he is recording and filming it because the broker owner is so pleased with the presentation, they're going to make it a training program for his company and he's on there. It's unbelievable.

You mentioned that you have chapters, so how does your consulting and coaching program work? Is there a limited number of people allowed in?

Yes, my consulting and coaching program is limited, and it's limited by the number of people I want to work with, frankly. Here's a life secret for the readers. I first picked out my ideal lifestyle and then went to work building it in that way. It's limited by how many people I want to coach, and there's only going to be a few.

The secret is not necessarily how much money you make. The real secret is choosing how much money you want and then having it delivered to you the way you want. You're a lot younger than I am. You're in a different place in your life. You may want something more than I do.

Once you have the system, you're the only one that determines how big, how small, how medium you want it. Does that make sense?

That makes total sense. Like you said, you're putting it in place and being able to have the lifestyle you want and get the things you want. If that's having your system bring you X amount of business per month, and that keeps you happy and keeps you in the position you want, then definitely.

Most people in the business that I know would be perfectly happy receiving 75 purchase transactions per year and having their clients refer business. You and I both know in this business, you can make a ton of money doing that.

My average revenue per year is $600,000. If you want to build a million dollar a year business in revenue, my system will show you how. If you'll be happy with a $300,000 a year gross revenue, my system will show you how. You're $300,000 and want to go to $750,000, my system shows you how.

That's great to be able to have that in place.

So, to share some of the secrets, your readers should consider—not just consider, but also embrace and do everything they can to work with realtors. The National Association of Realtors does a survey every couple of years, and I just bought the newest one that came out, went through it with a fine-toothed comb. I know more about what their survey does than 90 percent of their 1.3 million members. They don't even read it. It's full of marketing gold.

For a mortgage person, the gold in it is that 50 percent of all sellers use an agent for the next transaction they're buying, and less than 20 percent moved out of the area. If you're a person that's not licensed all across America, so what? You should still be working with realtors.

The next step that I thought was incredibly important for why mortgage people should make this a part of their business is that 52 percent of both buyers and sellers chose their realtor based on trustworthiness and honesty. That only comes from what others are saying about you.

Therefore, those people are telling me that is the number one reason they want somebody to help them. That comes down to character. How do you find out about character? Only what others are saying about you.

Testimonials are huge.

Testimonials are a must. My point is if you have 50 percent transactions being done by the same realtor, and he's in your herd, not only if he's working with a seller, there's a potential buyer for you right there 50 percent of the time.

So, the mortgage guy goes through and looks at how many houses are listed in his community. Say you have a thousand. That means if nothing else there's 500 buyers, and out of that 500 buyers, only 20 percent or fewer are going to move out of state. So there are 100. You have 400 purchase transactions going on right there. Who's getting that business?

Someone needs to be.

It should be us. It should be your readers.

How does your system work for company owners that are trying to find ways to drive business to their individual mortgage brokers?

That's a good question. It works this way. My business has gotten to a point that I have helpers on my team, junior mortgage brokers if you will, and so it's simple. In the community, the owner is attracting the realtors, and in their initial contact, the loan officer that he is going to assign or have work with this realtor is in that meeting.

To receive your $247 in free bonuses: www.TheInsiderSecretsGift.com

Everybody should have Goodwill Ambassadors. That's what I call my guy. He's a goodwill ambassador. When I'm done with you, I'm going in today because my goodwill ambassador has a new realtor coming for their orientation meeting, and I'm going to be telling that realtor all about the Pinnacle Club, all about the benefits, and all about why they must do business with us. At the same time, I'll have my goodwill ambassador there saying, "Okay, if you can't get me, this is who you get. If you can't get him, you get me."

Now, my goodwill ambassador has to be a service person for that individual, do all the other stuff that I used to do and follow up. It's just a matter of putting a tweak to the system.

I have my goodwill ambassador take care of the relationship with my member and when my member refers a loan, my goodwill ambassador works it. I oversee it. He is paid less and I make an override. So, I've actually created how to make an override out of your business.

There's another way you can do it—consumer direct. We did this in the '90s. We would run radio shows. We ran ads. We did all this jazz, and we brought in a whole bunch of phone calls, and we handed leads out to the loan officers and their job was to close them. That's having a sales force.

Many businesses operate that way right now. Business owners may not actually want to do loans themselves; they're running the companies that are trying to create leads and they're giving them all off to their loan officers or whatever. The same thing can be done here. Does that answer your question?

Yes, it does.

The system works for owner operators as well as individuals.

What's the best way for someone to reach out to you?

It's TracyTolleson.com. To find out more about my system, go there and request a personal letter.

Like you said earlier, most people don't really want to talk or deal with realtors, but your system takes all the guesswork out and makes working with realtors easy.

That is correct. The system allows you additional revenue or your only source of revenue. You can make this an addition to your business, and after a year or two of doing it, you may say, "This is the only way I want to do business," or you may say, "I like this and I like the other."

This system is something that even owners can get involved in and have their junior advisors in there as well. One system can just consistently grow the business.

In review, all mortgage businesses must understand that you have to have systems in place. Your readers should understand that they should have a system for lead generation, and I'm all about making that addition of lead generation through the realtor community.

All mortgage businesses must have systems in place to attract the lead, convert the lead and close the lead. All mortgage businesses need systems in place, back end systems, and this isn't some complicated thing. It's just consistency.

Mortgage businesses must move away from being totally dependent on refinances. Yet, at the same time, have systems in place never to miss the refinances.

I like my business system to be a triangle. At the top of

the triangle, I have realtor recruiting and recruiting system. At the left side of the triangle, I have a realtor retention system, and at the right side of the triangle, I have my client retention system.

All three of those work together so that the flow continues through feeding the other one. I have business I am getting from clients now that did not and will not go back to their original realtor that referred them in the first place.

I'm just a fool if I let that get away from me.

Now, we have proven that it is easily duplicated. The reader can know that it isn't just something that works for me. That's the neat part. Thank you for giving me this opportunity.

Chapter Six
Interview with Brad Cooper

Brad Cooper is a National Mortgage Expert, who uses radio and free publicity to generate a stream of borrowers wanting to work with him. By positioning himself as the expert, he has eliminated all the rate and fee questions that average mortgage brokers find themselves answering on every deal. Brad has become a celebrity instead of a commodity. He truly is a leader in our industry and you will want to read and learn from this very informative chapter.

Brad, please give us an idea of how you got your start in the mortgage business.

I've been in the business over 15 years. I have a criminal justice degree and I was a police officer for three years. I find that was valuable experience because in the past 15 years, a lot of my clientele (people I arrested) as a police officer were as nice as some of my past mortgage clients. The first 10 years I was like any other loan officer; I did traditional advertising, cold calling and really non-effective marketing for my business. About five years ago, things completely changed. I was introduced to Loan Officer Success. I shortly joined a coaching group and I learned how to be a marketer of my business. Around the same time, I discovered a different method of reaching prospects vs. traditional ways. That was through the introduction of radio and free publicity. I started my own radio show and quickly discovered that radio was an easy way to get my message out to tens of thousands of prospects, now positioning myself as an expert in the loan business.

I also discovered back then that to be different, to be successful, I was going to have to do something different from my competition. I looked around and every loan officer was doing the same thing—same advertising and the same loan programs. So I discovered a niche. I found my niche, which is helping families with credit issues including bankruptcies and foreclosures and helping them buy homes and refinance homes and get out of debt. Once I discovered my niche, I used radio as a resource to get my message out and quickly that positioned me as a local celebrity in my area. Shortly thereafter, I had a flood of prospects calling me begging me for my services. About that time I discovered, "I don't have to chase borrowers anymore. I don't have to worry about having the best rate in town, having the lowest closing costs." From that point on, my life had changed as a mortgage broker and loan officer forever. I owe a lot of my celebrity status to Loan Officer Success (www.loanofficersuccess.com), radio and other forms of free publicity.

It's such a unique product and niche that you have created for yourself. It's amazing to me that you developed radio shows as a way to generate business. You know the whole saying that there are riches in niches as opposed to being a generalist. How did you learn these things and position yourself as the expert?

To receive your $247 in free bonuses: www.TheInsiderSecretsGift.com

I tell my clients and other loans officers that I received my Ph.D. from the School of Hard Knocks so you can call me Dr. Cooper. I learned everything the hard way. I spent thousands of dollars and thousands of hours making mistakes to discover ways of making my life easier, my mortgage company's life easier and more profitable. Before I discovered radio and other forms of publicity, I was working 80 to 100 hours a week. I have a wife (Shelly) and two beautiful daughters (Grace and Maggie) and was never home. At that time, I took massive action with my radio show and other publicity strategies and made a decision to change.

I'll never forget my first radio show. I was scared to death. I am, for the most part, an introvert. I was scared to speak in front of groups of people. To be on the radio and talk to tens of thousands of people was very frightening. I said, if I'm going to stay in this business, I'm going to be different from other loan officers. Once I did it, it was so easy as far as talking and being interviewed and from that point on that opened up many other doors. Shortly thereafter, I had other radio stations contacting me for interviews. Secondly, local newspapers throughout the area started writing articles about me, our company and the niche I specialized in.

You said you had people writing articles about you as well after that. So it's stemmed out past radio. You would think that many times people want to come in and they always want you to spend large sums of money on marketing when they try to sell you. How much were you finding that you were spending on this product and getting this publicity?

Prior to me starting radio and doors opening for me, I spent tens of thousands of dollars in advertising for articles

To receive your $247 in free bonuses: www.TheInsiderSecretsGift.com

and other advertising methods. Just in the last several years, doing radio and other media opportunities: newspaper, other radio stations, television, and other publications would have been unaffordable, if I had to pay for it. I went back and calculated how much it would have cost Brad Cooper to pay all these resources that did basically all this advertising for free and it would have cost me hundreds of thousands of dollars to provide all the content for advertising. Wow, this was a big mindset change in my career as a loan officer.

I just had this recently happen to me. A local publication has a magazine they distribute monthly in our area. It goes out to over 100,000 homeowners. They asked me if I wanted to advertise. I said, "No, but I'll be more than willing and happy to write a short article in your publication for free to educate your readers." They took me up on that. So now, I have a small article in a publication that goes out to over 100,000 homeowners every month and the cost for me is zero. The return on investment (R.O.I.)—Priceless.

That's just amazing, that you're able to get all that free marketing and publicity by being knowledgeable. What type of things are you discussing on your radio show and columns to position yourself as an expert?

There are numerous topics to cover…I'll never forget when I started radio, I had the show manager I was dealing with say, "You know, Brad, what can you come up with as far as information topics week in and week out about mortgages? There's only so much you can talk about." It's just the opposite; I smiled and said, "You'll be surprised." Each week on my radio show, I go through various articles in newspapers and publications. There are unlimited topics to choose from. I often have weekly guests on my radio

To receive your $247 in free bonuses: www.TheInsiderSecretsGift.com

show from bankruptcy attorneys, appraisers, realtors, CPAs, financial planners, insurance agents and so on. Anything to do with financial services can make the conversation and the message educational and interesting. If you look around now, with the record amount of foreclosures and bankruptcies that are occurring, one out of three people, and I would say probably more like two out of three people nationwide, have some type of credit problem or credit issue. If not that, they have debt, so any message regarding what we do or what my guests talk about will hit probably 75 percent if not more of the radio audience.

That is great information for everyone and actually leads me to another question about how this creates consistency in a roller coaster industry where lenders and brokers are leaving at a rapid pace.

That's right. I've had several loan officers contact me in the last several months and say, "Brad, what are you going to do now? You know there have been over 60 lenders that have been sold or filed bankruptcy and lenders are changing their guidelines. Are you going to be changing your niche pretty soon and if so what are you going to change it to?" One thing I realized being in the business for 15 years, this is the fourth cycle I have experienced in a down economy. I get excited because we are going to see thousands and thousands of loan officers fall out of the business. The way I see it is less competition. When I'm doing my direct mail campaigns there's going to be less clutter that my prospects are going to have to go through because my competition is falling out of the business. I see opportunities, the time we're in right now is probably the greatest opportunity a loan officer will have to position themselves for the years

To receive your $247 in free bonuses: www.TheInsiderSecretsGift.com

to come when the market changes and we enter into a new refinance. We have a great opportunity as you look around, especially in my personal niche.

As you just mentioned, many people are going to be dropping out of this business, because they're doing what everyone else is doing. How can loan officers learn more about ways to position themselves as the experts in their own niche and local markets?

Most loan officers don't have a niche. Most loan officers try to be all things to all people. The first thing I would recommend is find a niche and when you're finding that niche, whether it's my niche, families with credit issues or maybe it's reverse mortgages, maybe it's first-time homebuyers, maybe it's commercial property or construction loans. Whatever that is, make sure you have a passion and a desire to help clients in that area.

So once you finally discover your niche and the passion, then the next part is just letting the world know about it. It's interesting, in my area, there are probably 15 mortgage companies within a two-mile radius and there are probably 50 banks within a mile radius. I don't see any of those as my competition. On the contrary, we refer business back and forth to each other. They know my niche is helping families with credit issues. I do not offer commercial loans. I do not offer construction loans. I do not offer loans in other niches so I refer business to them. So the big thing is, once you discover your niche, let the world know that you're the expert.

One way that I've had incredible success is through radio shows. That's the quickest way. Then writing articles for newspapers or other publications and not only that, leveraging those opportunities that I just discussed and implementing those into all your marketing strategies. For example, I do direct mail campaigns once a month and in all my direct mail campaigns, I have a picture of me at the radio station behind the studio with the headset on, showing and telling people I have my own radio show. Everybody who comes to my mortgage website—www.cooperfinancial.com—which is thousands of people a month, will see my picture at the radio station. There are many different ways of getting your message out there and many ways that are free and cost effective.

You are using many different mediums to get your message out, but how are you creating a massive appeal to people tuning in to your show and reading your columns?

It's crucial to always include in your message something that's interesting, never be boring. That's probably the biggest cardinal sin that a lot of loan officers, financial planners, and others make that are in newspapers or radio shows. You have to make it interesting. You have to make it fun and be yourself, be sincere; do not pretend to be someone you're not. When the public is reading or listening, they will notice that. Another thing that has probably been the biggest help for me is telling my own story. Ten years ago, I was bankrupt and living with my mother and father-in-law. That was an embarrassing and humbling time in my life. However, I share that story and the stress I went through, the ulcers, the sleepless nights, the marital problems and the list goes on. I share that with my listeners. I share that with the readers of my publications and instantly, there's a connection. Probably the number one advice I could give is tell your story and I often get the response, "Well, you have a story I don't." Everybody has a story and you have to discover what that story is, let others know it and instantly you'll see a connection.

To receive your $247 in free bonuses: www.TheInsiderSecretsGift.com

I've noticed when you tell a story, and I've talked to some of my clients about mine, I think it almost takes them off guard and let's them relax a little bit because they feel comfortable with you. They feel as if they know you now.

Absolutely. The niche that I am in and the clients I help are sometimes very embarrassed and humiliated. When a couple comes in my office, I can see the embarrassment and the sadness. The first thing I do and say is, "I know how you feel. I felt the same way. Here's what happened to me." Once I share my story, it's just like seeing the ice break, the tension in the air just breaking in half. Instantly they're sitting on the edge of their seat and there's an interest, there's a connection and the rest is simple.

That has helped in my business, I'm sure it will help our readers as well if they actually discover that as opposed to just coming in and talking business. Most brokers are trained to talk about rates and fees with people. The story helps create the personal relationship, while rates and fees turn you into a commodity.

That is so true. Another big thing, which I have done in the last four to five years, is knowing whom you want to work with. I work with people that are already sold on my services before they even come in to my office. So when I have an appointment I know the people are already sold on me and what I specialize in and they know that I'm an expert. They know that I'm different from everybody else. Probably 99 percent of the time, the issue of rates or fees rarely comes up as an objection. It's no different, this just happened to me last week. My wife was very ill. I had to take her to the emergency room. I had a choice to make. I could have gone to the Yellow Pages, called 12 hospitals in our area, and found out who was the cheapest and took her there because I wanted to save money. Instead, I knew who the best was, price wasn't an issue, and I went there. I just read an article where 95 percent of your prospects and your appointments are not so much fee or interest rate conscious as you think they are. Most people want value. They want to hear from you as an expert, but keep in mind as an expert, whether you've been in the business six months, six years or 20 years, you have to offer value.

What are some good pointers that mortgage brokers can do to add value besides keeping up on the industry?

Well that's one point. Another is investing in yourself and your education and keeping up on what's going on in the industry. I subscribe to all the mortgage publications so I have mind awareness. I don't spend hours and hours studying what's going on in the bond market and rates. However, I do educate myself and never stop learning.

Secondly, I go way beyond just the loan process with my clients. Assisting with their mortgage is really a small part of what we're talking about and discussing. Just to share with you a few things that I always share with our clients; number one is I'm not an accountant or a CPA but I do offer valuable information on the topics of tax refunds. I have several relationships with CPAs and accountants that I refer too. One of the biggest mistakes that most borrowers are making is they're getting back huge refunds. On average I've seen anywhere from $4,000 to $6,000. I teach them what a tax refund is, and that getting a refund is a mistake because it's an overpayment of taxes. Lastly, I show how our CPA or accountant can help them with adjusting their

W4 forms and now they get an extra $400, $500, $600 a month in their paychecks.

That's one area. Another area is we show families how to get out of debt usually in less than 10 years. We teach equity acceleration programs. We discuss, though I'm not an attorney, the basics and the importance of a trust. Life insurance is another area of education all of our clients receive. When they leave my office, normally their heads are spinning and they get a lot more than they even thought they're going to get. That's the wow feeling you should be giving to your prospects, appointments and clients when they leave your office. If you're not, you need to look at your presentation. I've used a tape recorder or a video camera to record myself with a client and that's an area you can improve upon. Just look at your message and ask yourself continuously, "What makes me different than everybody else?" That actually happened to me about 10 years ago. I had a client come in who was a high profile person in our community. He looked me in the eye and said, "Brad, why should I do business with Brad Cooper and Cooper Financial? What makes you different than the bank that I bank with?" You have to ask yourself that. If you can't answer that, you need to look at your business and if you still can't answer it, you may not be in the right business.

You are becoming much more than a mortgage broker to them and creating a relationship.

That's right; I'm looking at developing long-term relationships. I'm not like the average loan officer in our industry that makes a commission and moves on to the next client and never follows up again.

What types of things are you doing to automate your system and stay in front of your past clients and how many times do you touch them after closing to keep them as a client?

That's a great question. That's where most loan officers fail and I did for the first 10 years of my business. I have several systems in place now for clients and prospects that are not clients yet. Let me share with you several things I do currently: when we close a loan, within just a few days they get a gift from our office showing appreciation. Normally, that will be sent to the wife or girlfriend at their place of employment. That way all their co-workers and friends will be around and hear about the great experience they had with Cooper Financial.

Secondly, they're immediately enrolled in our monthly newsletter.

Thirdly, about a year ago I started implementing a monthly mailer. Every month they get a mortgage tip mailer, which is an inexpensive postcard that gives purely educational content. I'm keeping in front of my past clients on a monthly basis. In addition to mailers I am doing an e-mail blast to my past clients every week, which is called a Wednesday Morning Mortgage Tip. As soon as they come in Wednesday morning and open up their e-mail inbox, they will normally see an audio and video mortgage tip from me. Those are several areas where we reach our past clients. This leads me to this point. About five years ago, I noticed that a special publication I was getting monthly showed all the clients who refinanced or purchased a home every month. I reviewed this data and noticed a common trend, "Wow, this person was a past client of mine." On average I was seeing anywhere from five to seven of my clients that went through a different bank or a mortgage company monthly. I started to get aggravated and mad and then I started to think, "Well, why should they come back to me? I helped them with a loan and I never called them back. I never offered them anything after the closing and never called." That's when I immediately made the change.

Then on the other side of this, since we're on the topic of conversion and keeping in touch, we have clients that call in and we cannot help them right now because of credit issues or maybe timing. The timing may not be right, or maybe they're in the market of looking for a house and that could drag on for several months. We immediately enroll them in a conversion campaign, which is an 18-minute newsletter that we do monthly. In addition to that, they're getting copies of my radio show recordings once a month. They're getting articles I've written in other publications, a copy of that in the mail. Those unconverted leads are getting ongoing information from Brad Cooper, Cooper Financial, and when they are ready or when they do find a house, they're not going to go anywhere else. They're going to come back to our company because I took the time, effort, and a small expense of usually a stamp every month to follow up with them.

That is huge, because I know many people in the industry close that loan and they send their client maybe a thank you e-mail and that's usually the last time they talk to them and they just hope they get a phone call back. Longevity in this business is your past clients. A lot of business that you'll end up getting will be past clients or a referral business.

Absolutely. Talking about referrals, probably about 90 percent of our business the last several years have been either repeat business or referrals. The number one if not number two client I love and enjoy working with is a referral from one of my partners. I have relationships with CPAs, bankruptcy attorneys, financial planners and many more that results in about two or three closings per month in my business.

It's important to develop relationships with other partners whether it's CPAs, attorneys and so on. When you start out and you don't have any relationships right now, it's not going to happen overnight. When you do approach these contacts that you want to build relationships with, keep that in mind that you're going to have to go in and let them know what you can do for them and their business. Not what the traditional loan officer does, especially in the path of real estate agents. They go in with donuts and rate sheets and say, "We're the best. You need to send me business." It's not going to happen.

I'll share a simple strategy that caused an explosion in my business the last three years. This strategy is called cross marketing. This is what I mean by cross marketing. I have had a relationship with my CPA for about 10 years and just in the last three years, we were talking and I said, "You know what? You have a client database of over 1,500 clients that love you and they come back every year. I have a client database of over 1,000. Here's an idea I'll share with you. How about you endorse me and my company to your clients and I'll do the same for you to my clients?" So I personally prepared and wrote a simple endorsement letter about my services. I had my CPA review it and she okayed it. So the endorsement letter came from her, from her company and on her letterhead and stationary. I paid for the printer to prepare and mail it out. In return, we did the same thing for her with my clients. We do that on an ongoing basis and that amounts to several loans per month just from that one little concept of cross marketing with each other. Now I'm in the process of doing that with my financial planners, insurance agents, bankruptcy attorneys, trust and will attorneys and others.

There are so many different ways to bring in business and I don't think the people that we talked about earlier that are dropping out are the ones that are thinking outside the box and realizing they can get that done. I imagine you had some help during your career. Did you ever hire your own business coach and how has that helped you take your career to the next level?

About four years ago, I was introduced to mortgage coaching and my first coach, Reed Hoisington, who is a well-known mortgage coach and information marketer in the mortgage world. Shortly thereafter, I met Brian Sacks and Loan Officer Success, which changed my business and personal life forever—www.loanofficersuccess.com. I continue with coaching and being part of a mastermind-coaching group with other like-minded loan officers throughout the United States. This was probably the biggest turning point in my career. In my area, the only one I really share my business with is my wife. After a while, she gets tired of listening to it and I have no one to talk to. What I've discovered with a mastermind-coaching group is we're all like-minded. We all can share our successes and failures. We can find out what others are doing and use their ideas and we can share our ideas with other loan officers within the coaching group. This has made a huge impact in my business. Because of coaching, I continued my education and training through Loan Officer Success.

Two short years later, I became part owner and partner in Loan Officer Success with Ken Schreiber and Jessika Ondrick.

To receive your $247 in free bonuses: www.TheInsiderSecretsGift.com

Now I get the best of both worlds. I get to be on both sides of the fence. I get to still be a part of the mortgage world and originate loans daily. Then on the other side, I get to help other loan officers and coach them on how to be successful and maximize their profits and have a life.

I am in a few coaching programs and it has been a tremendous help growing my business and career. You are with like-minded people that are trying different things, trying to grow as individuals and grow their business as well. I've even discovered, if I could be a part of every coaching program, I think I would. I believe it is that beneficial.

You're right and to add to that, here's what I discovered with many loan officers, and I have a friend who's a loan officer in my area who is guilty. We do coaching; we educate loan officers throughout the United States. When we think of seminars and investing in CDs, DVDs, manuals, anything to further your education and make you a better loan officer, he views that as an expense. This is sad; to be successful and I would say probably one of the biggest reasons that loan officers fail is they don't look at this business as their career. They do not invest in themselves and when you stop investing in yourself, you will fail. You will not succeed in this business without coaching and education.

I found Loan Officer Success and signed up for the free e-mail newsletter that you provide. I purchased the gold package and when I received it, I ripped through it as if I was a kid on Christmas morning. I started reading, listening and watching all the material that comes with the program. Once I got halfway through it, I wondered why I had not found this before. It is amazing how much knowledge and information is out there that

successful people have already developed that can take away all the guesswork or trial and error to developing your business.

You're exactly right. You mentioned the gold system, which I had the great opportunity to invest in about four years ago. It helped my business tremendously but I...sad to say, I guess a confession. I didn't open it up as quickly as you did. I let it sit in the floor because I had a million other things going on and I had it on the floor as a doorstopper for six months. I looked around the office, I'm looking around my office now, and I have a system here. I probably invested over a quarter of a million dollars in systems in the last five years. I realized when I looked at the gold system six months later, after using it as a doorstopper, the insanity has to stop. Unless I make a change and start implementing, nothing is going to change. So I opened the box and it was just like a Christmas gift, like you said. I dove into it. My staff dove into it with me. We worked on it together and the key thing there is take action and implement.

Definitely! There is so much great knowledge in there, which leads me to another important question here for you. What is the best way for somebody to reach out to you if they want to learn more about these systems that you have put in place that have been so successful for you?

There are two different ways of reaching me for more information: number one, you can go to www.loanofficerpublicity.com for more information on how to create your own radio show and use publicity. In addition to radio, you will learn how to use free publicity whether it's books, newspaper articles, magazines, blogs or television, and quickly position yourself as a local expert and a local celebrity in your area.

For additional information and other valuable moneymaking marketing systems you can visit: www.loanofficersuccess.com or contact Brad at brad@loanofficersuccess.com.

I've implemented all the systems that we've talked about today that can be found at www.loanofficersuccess.com and at www.loanofficerpublicity.com. Life is awesome. I was talking earlier about working 80 to 100 hours a week before educating myself and investing in myself. Now I'm closing fewer loans per month than I was four or five years ago and the fun part about that is I'm making a lot more money. The best part about everything, especially if you would ask my wife or my two little girls, is they see me a lot more.

I'm working on average at about 25 hours a week making more money, closing fewer loans because I put systems in place. Whether I'm in my office on a regular basis or I'm out of my office, which is more common, my business will continue. As a loan officer, you need to be asking yourself this question. If you were gone for a month, would you still have a business when you got back in town? I look back the last 12 months and I looked at my schedule. I've been doing a lot of traveling the last couple years and last year there are three months out of the entire year collectively that I was not in my office nor in my house nor in my town. I was away on business and vacation and the months that I was gone, we had record earning revenue months. It all goes back to having the right systems in place and being able to implement. Several years ago, I learned a phrase from Brian Sacks—"Trust, But Verify." Having a great staff helps me have a successful business and be away, but you have to trust and verify things are being done.

To receive your $247 in free bonuses: www.TheInsiderSecretsGift.com

Having that freedom seems to contradict all other mortgage brokers beliefs. I worked 80-hour weeks and was a generalist to my clients, until I discovered systems. Once I started implementing my systems, it completely changed everything.

By having those systems in place, you can carry yourself to other people in our industry or any industry. It's quite hilarious. Every time I go through an airport, a mall, everyone's got a cell phone glued to their ear or they're checking e-mail through their iPod, Blackberry or Blueberry, whatever you call them, which I don't own. It's crazy that they try to be all things to all people. They're available seven days a week, 24 hours a day and that goes back and it's contrary to what we teach. We teach: find a niche, become an expert in that niche and let the world know about it. When you're an expert, you can set your own hours. You dictate and control your schedule. You no longer allow borrowers or prospects to dictate your schedule.

I only have two days a week and certain times that I will see clients. I have clients that drive as much as two hours one-way to see me. I don't take the excuses anymore, "I have to work." "I get off at six o'clock. I can't see you." I don't accept that anymore because if you were to go to a doctor, or have to have your license renewed, you would find time. Whether it's through lunch or break or take a day off, I'm frequently telling people, "Well, you need to take a vacation day." "You need to take a personal day." When you change your mindset and start having expectations of what your clients should do and you're controlling your schedule, that's when your business will explode.

What are some things that you would offer to the people that say I can't do that or it won't work for me?

If Brad Cooper can do it, anybody can do it. I'm not that bright. I do have an education but I barely got through high school. It's a miracle I even got through college. I just read an article that rated the mortgage industry below the used car industry. That was embarrassing because I've been in this business 15 years and I view myself as a professional. I guess the one message I would want to get out to a loan officer who's just now getting in to the business, maybe who's been in the business for six months, six years or maybe even 35 years. Look at yourself as a professional. Treat the business as a career and educate yourself. Find that niche, become that expert and let the world know about it and teach others to do that as well. That's the message I'm often telling loan officers because I see so many loan officers who've been in this business maybe a few months or a couple years and they're treating it as a part-time hobby. It's making us look bad, giving us a black eye. So I guess to sum up everything, I would say be a professional, invest in yourself, find a niche and have a passion, a love and a desire to help families. If you're missing that, leave the industry; go find something else to do.

That's great advice because if people aren't doing that, they should be. It makes things easier for us because it doesn't give mortgage professionals such a bad name when somebody doesn't like doing what they're doing so they just churn and burn a customer.

That's why earlier in our conversation we were talking about the economy changing and I said I was excited. The times where we're going through a down market, I call a mortgage storm. I recently heard Brian Sacks refer it to a mortgage enema. I get excited because it's weeding out all the bad apples. Anytime we go through a cycle and rates go down, everybody and their brother gets into the business. You know what? Selling used cars last week, I'm going to get in the mortgage business. I was a bricklayer last week, I think I'm going to become a mortgage loan officer because I can go out and make all this money in a short period.

During this flushing out period, we have all these loan officers who are not serious, who don't care about the prospects, who are in it for the wrong motives and wrong reasons. That's why I'm so excited and the time now is so exciting for business. I, our members, our coaching members and members within Loan Officer Success are having record income producing months; month in and month out because they're implementing the systems that we teach. That's the fun part; being through this down market before several times during the last 15 years, when you come out of this, you think you're doing great now, wait. Your business will quadruple when the market changes.

Absolutely. You have the knowledge and you work your system and you are definitely the expert. Thank you so much for your time today, Brad. It was definitely informative and our readers will learn from this interview.

My pleasure and I wish you the best of success. Remember that it all goes back to coaching; it's surrounding yourself with people that are better than you are.

CHAPTER SEVEN

INTERVIEW WITH ANDY LOCKWOOD

ANDY LOCKWOOD has created a highly profitable career as a Mortgage Broker. He owns and operates a very successful one-man mortgage operation in Weston, Florida.

Andy doesn't employ any loan officers and creates income levels that are unbelievable to an ordinary broker in the mortgage industry. He has contributed to *The Scotsman Guide* and *NARLO Today*; both are highly respected publications in the Mortgage Industry.

Andy has decided to share his knowledge and Insider Secrets to creating a successful and profitable career as a mortgage broker. You will learn that no matter what the market is like, you can always have clients calling you to do business if you employ tested and proven direct marketing principles.

How did you get in to the mortgage business and how have you developed it over time?

Like many people who get into the mortgage business, I had no desire and I didn't grow up wanting to be a mortgage guy, I just stumbled into it. So I was actually—not that I'm proud of this, but—I was a practicing attorney working for a financial services company. Along the way, like many other financial services companies, we formed a mortgage lender. Because I was the geek who could take tests, I became head of the mortgage lender in the late '90s. Then the stock market took a dump, and the bubble burst, the .com world and all that, so companies like mine, small publicly-traded companies, had problems. We were bought out by one company, then we were bought out again, and it was going to keep happening. After the second time, I had a choice of trying to stick around with the new owners, or trying to do something on my own to protect myself. I took a shot at going into business for myself. I was looking for opportunities, and I could form my own stock brokerage company, which I had no desire to do. But I had learned a little bit about the mortgage business along the way, so I figured why not take a shot at that. So it was that arbitrary almost. I got very lucky because of all the refinancing that started happening in the early 2000s. That's how I got into the business; it wasn't my master plan.

Now, it's a one-man show. I used to have 15, 20 guys working for me pounding phones, but that turned out to be a loser both economically and time-wise because it was a lot of babysitting, it was a lot of needy people, working Internet leads, and all that. Over a year ago I got rid of everybody, after I came back from a month-and-a-half vacation where I was stewing about how many losers I had working for me.

Doing that takes up a lot of brainpower.

Yes, energy, mental energy, plus the physical, plus the amount of time. So I got rid of everybody and scaled down into an executive suite, literally one office. My gross numbers are up, of course my net numbers are way up, and my overall quality of life and time, and all that, has vastly improved.

You mentioned that you provided Internet leads for people to work. How did you restructure bringing in your own leads if you got rid of those?

I had never personally worked on Internet leads myself. I had always been a face-to-face, belly-to-belly working type of guy. I told you I was an attorney so I had a bunch of yuppie friends, CPAs, lawyers, whatever. I would just go out and pound the pavement having lunch with them, or going to those dumb little networking meetings, like Chamber of Commerce, all that junk where you give your elevator speech 50 times a week. You run up to realtors and say, "Hey, get to know me, I have a loan for you." I gradually realized I was really heading for burnout because I was working all the time. At the time, we had two kids. I was one of these annoying guys on the soccer fields, not really watching my kids; I was on the phone trying to revive some sort of mortgage emergency at any given time, and was heading toward burnout.

I knew there had to be a better way but I didn't know what it was. I'd actually had a bad experience in my first foray into advertising. When I was in-house counsel, before I made the jump to self-employment, the financial services company I worked for raised about eight million bucks through the public markets in a small offering. But the mandate was to promote ourselves. Down here in Florida, we were looking for a celebrity who would stand for solid, smart, intellectual, successful person who was well known to represent a financial services company. We ended up landing Don Shula, which was neat because he is—I don't know if everyone knows who he is—but he's won the most

NFL games out of any head coach, and he's the only coach in any major professional sport to have an undefeated season; he holds a bunch of records.

I'm sure he's well known in Florida.

He's like a God down here. We landed him and we paid an inordinate amount of money out of the public offering proceeds to land him. Then the question was, okay, now we have him signed, what do we do with him to bring in business? Then we promptly blew more than a million dollars hiring consultants and ad agents like a fancy South Beach, they-all-wore-black type of ad agency. I had no advertising experience whatsoever, but no one else wanted to step up so they threw it on my lap, the geek attorney, to try to handle it. The one cool thing is that the actual contract that we signed with Shula is signed by me. So somewhere out there there's a contract signed by both of us. That's my one claim to fame. But we spent all this money and we did all this advertising and printed up all these fancy brochures and collateral material and then sat back and waited for the phone to ring and it really didn't. We hardly got any business at all out of it. We had a lame sales force to begin with, older semi-retired guys, and the stereotypical South Florida guys.

So that was really my background. I knew that advertising and marketing worked for some people, but I didn't know how to do it. Then one day a friend of mine dumped a whole box of stuff on me and inside I stumbled across a newsletter written by Gary Halbert, who I'm sure you've heard of. It was a great sales letter, I didn't know what it was called at the time, but it was totally different from anything I'd ever read about marketing. That little letter really turned me on to a whole world of direct, emotional response marketing.

Fast forward three years later, once I started implementing that, my life changed. It's dramatically different and I realized that marketing could work.

You changed your marketing from pounding the streets to direct response marketing.

Yes.

How did it specifically change your business and the way you lived your life?

I don't usually use words like this, but it totally and radically changed everything. I see people who advertise these techniques and talk about the secret tactics, and so on and so forth. This stuff has been around since I think the Civil War; it's not new, and it's worked through all types of economic environments, wars, depressions, recessions, bad stock markets, good stock markets, and more. Once I figured out how to use it, almost everything I did became on autopilot because I know that if I get out X amount of marketing in a month, then 45 to 50, 60 days later I'm going to receive Y in commissions. It helped me predict almost to the dollar how much I'm going to make. I know exactly what's working and what's not working. I severely cut down on the amount of hours that I was putting into my mortgage business, so it's now something like 15 to 25 hours a week. Totally changed everything! Now I have four kids, so I'm even busier on the home front. I'm never on the cell phone with deals or emergencies when I'm coaching basketball, or hockey, or gymnastics, or whatever; it totally changed my whole life.

I imagine you meet many people out there that are doing everything that their competition is doing and they're working 50, 60-hour weeks and they're probably closing 15 to maybe

To receive your $247 in free bonuses: www.TheInsiderSecretsGift.com

$20,000 per month if they're good. What type of fees are you finding yourself doing on a 15 to 20-hour week?

Well, because I'm marketing for specific types of deals, I may be able to maximize fees on this particular niche. So that's really helped me. I'm not doing more loans; I'm actually doing fewer loans. On average, the aggregate commission on any given month is about $50,000.

That's a big number for working 60 hours during the whole month.

I probably work less, but I'm just embarrassed to really admit it. Because I have my assistant handle most of it, and I have everything outsourced and systematized. My goal is to spend 100 percent of my time just meeting with clients or speaking to them on the phone. It doesn't quite work out that way all the time, but once you confine your activities to the most productive things and forget about all the other stuff, you really see time savings.

Definitely. Systems are a big thing for anyone to be successful, so how did you start developing your automated system?

Well, the first thing is basic; you need to have a system, because I didn't have one before. Before I had to get up, run out, introduce myself to people and shake hands, which I just hated doing. I was not that type of person to begin with, so just the realization that you need a system is one thing. One big influence, not so much on the mortgage side but just thinking about business in general, was the book *The E-Myth*; have you heard of that book?

Yes, I have.

It's a great book; I recommend it to you and everybody who is reading your book. It's by Michael Gerber and is really one of the central books in business thinking that many people have swiped. I'm not going to give you a book report on it. The main thing that I personally took away from it is that when you are in business, whether you're a huge multinational corporation or just a guy humping logs by yourself, there are really three basic roles that are played in any company. The main role is that of the shareholder or the owner and that's someone who thinks of strategy, marketing, ways of bringing in business. Then you have the technician, who is the person that actually does the work, so it's either application taking, processing, or getting mailers out, whatever, and then in the middle between those two roles is the manager who allocates the workload for the technicians.

Like I said, when you're an entrepreneur, a one-man show, you're wearing all three hats. The challenges that Gerber says is that you should be spending at least 80 percent of your time at the shareholder, strategist, or business owner level, which is a real eye-opener to me. So that means that all the other stuff that happens, like all the technical stuff, the management stuff, you should be off-loading as quickly as possible to somebody competent, or to more than one person that's competent. That was really the main thing that slapped me in the face. That was before I actually came across the direct marketing materials that I mentioned before. Because I remember thinking well, now I know I need to be spending 80 percent of my time on marketing, but what do I do? Then I came across this Halbert letter, and I came across people like Brian Sacks and Dan Kennedy, Bob Bly just led me on this three-year quest to soak up everything I possibly could on direct marketing.

With everything you're doing, did you find anything that's different, or are you doing anything special that others are not?

Well, it doesn't feel particularly special when I do it, like I said, I feel a little guilty about it. Sometimes it's a little easy. The main thing is systematizing and having everything running in place. There are always things to tweak and mailers that don't get out in a day that you want to get out. But what I'm really doing is all the stuff I'm describing—this is a cliché, but—I'm working on my business, not in my business. I'm working on the systems, I'm making sure that things are running relatively smoothly, and I'm just letting them happen. I'm letting the marketing get out, I'm letting the people call, and I'm letting the follow-ups happen. When the time is right in the sequence of people that are in my marketing funnel, I speak to them and then hopefully convert them. So it is different than many people because what they do—and I'm not putting anyone down because I did exactly the same thing—is they run out and try to grab about anything and bring it in the door. The opposite is to figure out what you want to bring in the door first; i.e., a niche, and then figure out how to get more of that business and bring it in.

You just mentioned a niche. I know many mortgage brokers feel they need to service every client. They don't really ever focus on just one niche and they're trying to be generalists. They're just out there trying to do everything for everyone, so how has really defining a niche for yourself helped you out?

Well, like you said, if you're going to be just another voice screaming, "I can do everything, no doc loans, no verification for national, how to present financing, blah, blah, blah," you look through the Yellow Pages, and you see the same ad over and over and over again. You have to ask yourself, why would someone pick you as compared to the guy two pages over, the guy two pages before you, it's the same stuff over and over again. The only reason that someone might pick you is that they're hoping that you're the lowest-priced guy. So once you compete on price you're going to lose because you're just a commodity, you're like a gallon of milk that can be picked up at the supermarket, or the gas station, or whatever. When you focus on a niche, you become a specialist. One of the most common analogies is like a specialist doctor, or heart doctor. If you need specialized care or if you have a heart problem, you're not going to whip open the Yellow Pages and find someone who is going to do open heart surgery for 50 bucks. Instead, you get a recommendation for the best care that you possibly can get, and you're not really going to question price at all. So focus on a niche, and there are plenty of niches out there. I found one particular niche that's very profitable for me where I've set myself up as the guru, as the guy on the hill, that has allowed me to command maximum fees, not argue with people about fees, and set my own schedule and have them conform to me.

You have picked a unique niche that most people don't even want to go near. Your niche is with homeowners who have a Chapter 13 bankruptcy. How did you start marketing for people in this niche and what's so appealing about it to you?

The second part of that question is easy. The thing that's so appealing to me is that I can make a lot of money on each deal and the people are extremely motivated to let me help them. I mentioned Gary Halbert before, he talks about marketing to a small pond of hungry fish. It's much better to focus your efforts on people who are motivated to use your

To receive your $247 in free bonuses: www.TheInsiderSecretsGift.com

services. Whether they know it or not, they have a problem, and you have to demonstrate that you're the person to solve it. So that part is easy, that's what I get out of it. In terms of how I got into it, that's yet another example of me stumbling around and not having any type of master plan, so it might be the theme of this interview. Again, I was trying to take anything that came in the door and networking with a friend who was a bankruptcy attorney, he's now more of a personal injury attorney, but we're close friends and he started referring me to some of his clients who were in Chapter 13 bankruptcies. I would take anything that came in the door. I completely screwed up the first couple, so they really were painful because I didn't know what I was doing.

By the way, I didn't really think about charging correctly for my services. I knew that it was different from A paper, but I was still getting fees similar to A paper, which was a big, stupid mistake that I made. A paper clients would beat me up over an eighth of a point even though they agreed to it and were locked in. The people who were in the bankruptcies were incredibly grateful to have me work with them. They were in disbelief that I could actually help them. It was a completely different type of dynamic. They respected whatever I recommended to them, they didn't really question it. Like I said, I was undercharging but once I started bringing up my fees they still didn't question my fees, so it turned out to be a lucky thing.

What I then did was sit down and figure out, well, how else can I bring in more of this type of business rather than just random referrals? One day I stumbled across—again, another stumble—I came across a tactic that I think I got out of one of Brian Sacks' products, his original goal system, which I think he still offers. He describes a tactic where you would just have someone send out an endorsement letter to their list, to their group of clients. So I talked my friend into doing that. He provided a list of maybe 50 people in a Chapter 13 and we sent out a letter on his letterhead that I had drafted and tried to bring him some business. That was really my first foray into direct response marketing.

How did that go for you?

It was unbelievable. I still wish I could get these results as consistently. For about $19 worth of postage and no other cost, I closed five deals. The deals converted to around $35,000 in fees. Again, this is before I started charging as much as I charge now. I probably left a lot of money on the table. However, for $19 we grossed like $35,000.

That's amazing for closing five deals at $35,000 in revenue. Many loan officers reading this book might think that's impossible, but you are living proof that good marketing can create a great response.

It was a great response. As I said, I've been trying to duplicate that, I've been trying to beat that ever since, and it was an endorsement letter. I've done a few similar campaigns like that, and that's actually part of my system. But it was a nice start to my life as a direct marketer.

What type of follow-up did you do with these clients?

That's another dumb thing. I did nothing. So, in a word, zilch. It was lame. I was still learning how to direct market. Again, I left money on the table, turned the fees, I left money on the table in terms of response because I should have been sending sequential mailers to these clients and I only sent one out. It is embarrassing but true.

Some marketers recommend touching clients seven times.

There are all these rules of marketing that float around online or in books. When I run a campaign now, with a variety of techniques, if I'm getting in front of them fewer than 7 to 10 times there's something wrong. Between mailers, voice broadcasts, follow-up mailers, and other things, the whole key is to keep after them.

Definitely. You are doing your direct marketing to Chapter 13 Bankruptcies, but there are different types of bankruptcies. So what exactly is a Chapter 13 compared to other types of BK?

That's a good question. A Chapter 13 is a repayment plan. For example, if you have $100,000 worth of debts that you can't pay and you file bankruptcy you have two choices. One, you can just wipe the whole thing out, and that's a Chapter 7. That is now harder than ever to be able to do because the laws changed in October of 2005, so now you have to qualify to file a Chapter 7 and wipe everything away. The opposite, for purposes of our discussion, is a Chapter 13 where that $100,000 gets converted into a repayment plan where much of it's written off, so maybe it's $60,000 and it's repaid over a five-year period. When you're looking at restructuring somebody's debts, meaning that you're taking the equity out of their house to pay off a Chapter 13 bankruptcy, you are taking that $60,000, and instead of it being paid over five years, you're now spreading it out over 30. It's almost a sure win-win when you are talking to a client and showing them their current payments and what they will be. They're very rate-insensitive.

Rate-insensitive?

They don't care about the interest rates as much as they care about the payments. So you can get away with a high interest rate and make maximum yield spread because you are drastically cutting down their monthly payments between their mortgage and the Chapter 13, converting that all into a mortgage, you're saving them hundreds, sometimes more than $1,000 a month right off the bat. The presentation that I do, which is simple, sells itself. You can be the world's worst salesman, I don't consider myself such a great salesperson, and the numbers will just speak for themselves.

It's amazing, too, that you can charge a higher rate and still be thanked for your business as opposed to like you said you used to work with the A paper clients who beat you up on an eighth of a point and are rarely ever satisfied.

It's about doing something beneficial for the clients. My theory is that people ask me questions about rates and fees because they're just conditioned that way, they don't know any better, they don't know all the questions to ask. So it's your duty to show them here are the benefits, here's really what we're going to be accomplishing. This is what you're paying now; this is what you will be paying after. That's just part of it. There are all sorts of other benefits that are important that I've discovered over the years of working with this type of client. Being in a Chapter 13 bankruptcy takes a severe emotional toll on the person; every expense, every bit of income is scrutinized by the Court, it's almost like having a parole officer. I've heard that more than once. They can't save for retirement; they can't allocate money for their kids' college education. There's a whole bunch of restrictions placed on them. There is a dramatic emotional toll that's on these people. You'll help them clean up their credit. There's a list of other things that they really want to do.

Do you find that the people you are working with are usually sold on you, your services and want to work with you because you have become the GURU by developing your own niche?

Yes. By the time I actually speak to someone, they've worked through what I need them to work through, which is a combination of my initial mailers to generate leads. Once they're in my marketing funnel, they will continue to get other things that support me in that guru status that I try to create for myself through a variety of strategies. So typically by the time I actually sit down with them face-to-face, which I try to do, it's not always face-to-face, but either on the phone or in person, then they're just ready to sign. Their decision has already been made and they're already pre-sold on me. Then the numbers speak for themselves, too, so it's really a lay-up.

It is a great feeling to have someone pre-sold on you, because that eliminates the chasing and hard selling of clients that don't really want to work with you.

It's a system to get them to be pre-sold on you. So you can spend virtually all of your time working with clients who've already raised their hands and said that they're interested in you.

When you get these clients in the door and they're interested and they're ready to move forward, how hard are these deals to do? I know many loan officers out there just avoid bankruptcy clients and do not want to work with them. Are these deals that difficult to get done processing-wise, or even placement?

Well, I'll be candid. They're not as easy as an A paper refinance. As I said before, the first few deals that I did I totally screwed up. Forget about all the typical reasons prime deals fail, because that's a whole other ball of wax. The reason a bankruptcy buy-out deal fails is really tied to the type of information you get up front from the courts and the attorneys and your ability to navigate through that group of players in the transaction. If you can have a good checklist and a good understanding of how to do that, you will eliminate 99 percent of the problems up-front. What I've done internally is come up with a system at work on how to eliminate those 99 percent. Once you do that and you have a good representative, a good lender, you have a good processor, and you have a decent understanding of how everything should work and how the deal should flow, it's very easy.

As you stated, it's about having the right team surrounding you to get these deals done and the right system. There have been many people out there jumping out of the business due to the recent so-called subprime meltdown. Has this hurt your ability to get these deals done?

Knock on wood, not at all. I actually think it might have the opposite effect. These deals are, in many ways, less risky for subprime lenders, so most of them will do these deals. The reason I'm saying they're less risky is when you think about it, you are doing a few things. You are, in general, coming up with low loan-to-value deals. I teach a certain method to market to people in the process where they have some time where they've built up equity. More important, the main reason people file a Chapter 13 bankruptcy is to protect their home equity, so they had some to begin with. So, number one, you're looking at a low LTV, low loan-to-value type of deal. The second thing is that these deals are mostly full documentation. When you file a bankruptcy, you're disclosing all sorts of financial stuff about yourself.

That's all part of the public records, and the underwriters are generally going to look at everything. Third, you're clearly benefiting the borrower; you're lowering their payments substantially. So it's a deal that most subprime lenders want. It's not one of these 100 percent stated income 580 type deals where they are all paying the price for doing those. These are deals where all the characteristics I've described are present and the borrower has established a good pay history at the higher level so now you're coming in and giving them a lower payment overall, it's a no-brainer, it's a slam dunk for the underwriter to approve it.

Which makes it easier, like you said; they're not the 100 percent stated deals, like everyone else is trying to do. What's the marketplace for this type of prospect? Didn't the recent change in the laws affect filings?

Well, they did; that was in October of 2005. Before the laws changed, when it was easier to file a Chapter 7, the courthouses across the country literally had people lined up around the block at all hours to file before that window closed. So the levels of Chapter 13s after that, the first quarter of 2006, were artificially depressed. What has happened, though—and I apologize, I don't have these numbers in front of me, but—the amount of filings has increased steadily from quarter-to-quarter-to-quarter so much that most experts now, most the bankruptcy attorneys, and the American Bankruptcy Institute are predicting that the filings are going to exceed their previous levels on a Chapter 13. The other key indicator is that the percentage of Chapter 13s compared to Chapter 7s is shifting much more in favor of the Chapter 13s just because of what I just mentioned; it's so much harder to file a Chapter 7 than it is a Chapter 13.

There are many favorable trends operating to make this to what I consider a ground-floor opportunity all over again. If you look at the things that drive bankruptcies in general—high consumer debt, inability to make a mortgage payment, divorce, all that type of stuff—there's really no reason any of that is going to do anything other than accelerate. Foreclosures are another key indicator. The foreclosure numbers are doubling virtually year-after-year. So the more bad stuff that's happening in the mortgage with the subprime adjustable rates adjusting, and people not being able to afford and go into foreclosure, the better it is for people pursuing this niche of Chapter 13 bankruptcy.

We've talked a lot here already today about the Chapter 13 Bankruptcy Buy-Out niche that you have, and the success you've had with it. In developing this system, there are probably a few trials and errors you've done. What type of failures and obstacles have you overcome to make yourself more successful, and what type of mindset have you had during all of this?

That's a very good question. My last biggest obstacle was having a huge office and many people working for me. That took awhile to get out from under, because I was buying Internet leads and spending a lot of time dealing with these losers. That was one obstacle that was easy to overcome, once I decided to get rid of it. However, with direct marketing, you have to test everything. I learned that sometimes the materials that I had labored over, that I thought were going to be the best, provided the worse response and vice versa. Sometimes stuff that I sent out thinking, "Okay, I'll give it a shot," turned out to be a huge winner. Learning how to test and stepping out from your own set of personal biases and prejudices was a big obstacle I didn't realize I had at the time.

Before I started doing this stuff, I thought there's no way it works. I would never open this type of mail, I would never respond to this. However, what I was really overlooking was that I'm not my target audience. I'm not marketing for Andy Lockwood; I'm marketing for people in a completely different type of scenario. That was a huge obstacle, too, understanding that I was not really the correct target. Other than that, it's just having the fortitude to come up with money to give these things a fair shot. That was an early battle that I had. The reluctance, I guess, to spend the money and try something. That was more of a mental thing.

I'm sure even throughout your whole career, too, the industry is full of ups and downs, as well. What things have you done that have allowed you to keep your focus on your main goals in dealing with the fluctuating mortgage industry?

It all relates back to what we've been talking about. I've had a system and it's produced results and I've just kept it going. Because over the course of six or seven mailers, for example, you're going to have good response and bad response, but you don't give up after you get a bad response, you keep mailing. The neat thing about the mortgage business is that one deal that you close can more than pay for a lot of marketing investment. So it would be a big mistake to give up too early when you don't get response. I've constantly made myself focus that there's still some life left in this list and I'm going to get those deals I want to get.

I've asked everyone that I've talked to this, because everyone always wants to know what the most successful people are doing. If someone's trying to learn the business then obviously Andy Lockwood is one of the most successful mortgage brokers in the industry here. What type of stuff are you reading?

To receive your $247 in free bonuses: www.TheInsiderSecretsGift.com

I read everything I can get my hands on.

You mentioned Michael Gerber and Dan Kennedy earlier.

I read everything I can get my hands on, and mostly not mortgage related. I'll read anything by either of those authors, as you just mentioned, Gerber and Kennedy, Robert Bly. I'm just looking at my bookshelf right now. Victor Schwab, Charles Oglivy, and Claude Hopkins. You can go on Amazon and just punch in direct marketing, or direct mail or marketing, and you'll come up with more than enough to get you going. I also invest in my education. I go to seminars, they cost time, and I'm not afraid to do it. I don't love the traveling at all, especially in today's particular airport security environment. And I'm very busy with the family. But I do it because it's important. So I'm always looking for, not necessarily the next greatest new idea, but I'm looking for either the same idea but just described a little bit differently to me because it might just resonate a little different, I might relate to it a little bit differently. I'm also looking to see what other people are doing to apply these principles that, like I said, have been around for more than a century. Sometimes I can hear the same thing repeatedly for a year and not really focus on it. Then, for whatever reason, something clicks, which can set off a very profitable idea.

I just went to a conference a couple weeks ago and I had that exact same experience. I was sitting there, joking with a friend, we were talking to each other saying this is so much different from the last conference, because this time we learned hey, pick a niche, because I say the same thing a lot, conference after conference. But that's not the point. The point is that if you come away with one thing, or you come up with something that's a principle that you certainly have internalized but someone else is using it differently and you can make money doing that, then it's more than worth the investment in money and time.

In coming back to that, what's the best way for them to reach out to you to learn the system you have put together that will allow them to increase their profits, and what are some of the major benefits they would get from looking into your system?

Well, I have a special site for your readers. It's www.MortgageMarketingWhiz.com/isb. That is the description of my bankruptcy buy-out riches marketing implementation system. It really is my bread and butter. I repackaged my own internal system into something that anybody can use. So we have a combination of a bunch of different things. We have six modules recorded on disk that are each about an hour, hour-and-a-half. They are joined by a whole bunch of marketing materials, which are the materials that are in the values day in and day out. You also get a Word disk so you can edit the documents yourself. Then there are many other bonuses.

Would you like me just to run through the title of each module and what's covered?

Let's do that so everyone has an idea.

The first module is called "How to Immediately Jump Start Your Production to Levels You Never Thought Possible Through Marketing to Homeowners in Chapter 13 Bankruptcies." It is the fast-start overview for those people who are somewhat hyper and want to get going immediately. I include myself as one of those people.

The second module is "Who Are Your Chapter 13 Prospects and What Do They Have in Common. How To

Find Them and Communicate to Them." That's a module about the psychographic way to find these prospects, what do they have in common, what are their common fears and problems and how do you communicate to them.

Then the third module, which is my favorite, is called "The Secret Power of Direct Mail Advance Copywriting Techniques to Market to Chapter 13 Homeowners." I probably could have spent a couple of days just talking about copyrighting, but we try to cram it into about 90 minutes. That's a really good module.

The fourth module is called "Systems to Create Leverage." That's where I give everybody names and what they should be looking for in terms of the vendors that I personally trust to use for all my campaigns, whether off-line or online.

Then the fifth module, I guess it's my least favorite, because it's the module where I talk about all the mistakes you make. We came up with the material for this module by looking at the deals that fell through our fingers. This module represents about $70,000 worth of lost commission, so it was very painful. It's called "Navigating a Deal: What You Must Know About the Bankruptcy Courts, Trustees, Attorneys, Paralegals, and Title Companies." The top 10 errors—I think we came up with much more than that—and how to avoid them and save tens of thousands of dollars. That's one that I pretty much insist that people have their processor listen to. Because you get them to eyeball some of these problems in advance and you will save yourself stress and you'll save yourself money.

Module six, the last module, is "The Top Six Objections From Prospects and How To Overcome Them," but I think we came up with about 10. I had a friend, Ken Schreiber, on that call, also, and we went back and forth, role playing and talking about how you overcome these objections and a different way to avoid them all together before they're even verbalized to you.

Is there any last piece of great advice that you would like to give to our readers as one of the most successful people in our industry?

Obviously pay close attention to what everyone is saying, the common things that are being covered by everybody that you're interviewing. Then understand that if you really want to do well, you need to devise a system. Whether it's investing in mine, or coming up with your own, or investing in somebody else's, you can't be afraid to put in not just the money but the time and the blood, sweat and tears into working on your business. If you don't work on your business then you'll never achieve anything close to what you're capable of doing. So many people in this business are stuck in the forest and the trees type of thing. They're not able to elevate themselves out of that and see the big picture. I think that's the most common mistake that I see people doing—in the weeds, slugging it out day-to-day and they don't have any prospects after getting out.

That's huge, because prospects turn into clients. Fantastic. Andy, I want to thank you so much for your time. It's been extremely knowledgeable for everyone. I'm sure that people will strive to reach the success that you already have reached.

All right, my pleasure. I enjoyed our conversation and hope your readers found it valuable.

Chapter Eight

Interview with Sue Haviland

Sue Haviland has taken a unique niche, ran with it, and has done some amazing things. It will be great for our readers to learn about this rapidly growing market. Sue generates a very large income by focusing on the reverse mortgage business. She's been in the industry for over 20 years and has created a system that generates reverse mortgage leads and clients, which is one of the most underserved and fastest growing markets for mortgage brokers.

You've done so many great things and I don't want to miss anything, so please let our readers now how you got to the point of becoming a national expert in the mortgage business.

I've been in the mortgage business for a little over 20 years. I actually started out taking applications, literally, learning the business from the ground up which, in hindsight, was a very good way to learn the business. It gave me insights from several different perspectives. I went on to processing and I actually had my greatest learning experience processing for Brian Sacks, who was a top producing loan officer and trainer, as you are probably familiar. Boy, processing for Brian was really a life-changing experience for sure.

While I was working with Brian, I let him know that I had an interest in learning how to originate, so he agreed to mentor me and helped me learn to be an originator with the systems that he had put in place and, as I was learning origination, came across some reverse mortgage articles. Now, keep in mind that this is quite a few years ago when there wasn't a whole lot out there about reverse mortgages. I was intrigued by the concept and I knew that we were going to be facing a growing senior population before too many years went by, so I continued to look for other resources and things to learn about reverses and I just became determined to read everything I could. Along the way, lo' and behold, one day I was working with a senior citizen couple who wanted to do a refinance, but unfortunately, their income did not permit them to do what they wanted to do. In addition, they had some impaired credit caused by the husband's medical issues. He had to miss quite a bit of work and they had some credit challenges.

It was then that I decided that the reverse mortgage was going to be the solution for these folks. I was going to commit myself to become the expert in this program, learn everything I could, and take this thing and run with it. I have never looked back. It's been an extremely rewarding experience working with this population and, after I had been doing reverses for a while, I realized that there wasn't a whole lot of training and systems out there. Brian always encouraged me to systematize everything that I did, so I decided to put something together myself. I thought, this reverse mortgages niche offers a terrific opportunity, but no other loan officer should have to learn it by trial-by-fire the way that I did. So I put together my Reverse Mortgage Success System, which will allow loan officers who want to originate reverse mortgages to do so, working in this fast-growing niche that exists within our senior citizen population.

Especially with the senior population and some of the challenges that they face, that's why this is such a great product.

Oh, yes. Reverse mortgages, for anyone who doesn't have a whole lot of exposure, allow senior homeowners age 62 and over to tap a portion of their equity and use those funds for practically any purpose and they never have to make a payment on that money as long as they live in the house. It's a unique loan program geared towards these senior homeowners. When we look at the rapid growth, the almost exponential growth in the senior citizen population today—the baby boomers are just now entering their retirement years—the program may have arrived just in time. Many of these folks are having some real income issues and living on a fixed income.

It's been reported that about 90 percent of our country's seniors rely on Social Security in some form just to meet their monthly obligation. That is a significant portion of our senior population relying every month on Social Security. So these folks who are living on these fixed incomes are finding that the money is just not meeting their needs, and many are even resorting to credit cards to meet monthly expenditures. We also have some folks who have had their pensions either reduced or, in some cases, eliminated along with medical benefits that were to accompany those pensions. These seniors planned their retirement with the understanding that these benefits would be there for them, and it is a rude awakening when they are cut.

So, they're feeling the squeeze, I guess you could say, from both sides—from an income standpoint where it's not meeting their needs, coupled with the fact that expenses are constantly rising. Things like medical expenses, prescription medication co-pays—even if they have coverage, they still have co-pays—rising real estate taxes, rising home maintenance expenses, all of these things are affecting our seniors in a very real way.

The elder generation had the goal to buy a home and pay it off, so I imagine that there is plenty of equity to work with. As you stated, this is a fast-growing market, so what potential do mortgage brokers have in this niche market?

The potential for the reverse mortgage market is unprecedented and I want to touch on something you mentioned about people that bought their home, stayed there for a long time, really didn't move, because, yes, that was the goal. Then when you bought your home, you got a mortgage; you worked like a dog to pay that mortgage off because it was a negative thing to have a mortgage. Some of our folks might remember mortgage burning parties. That was a big goal, to get rid of your mortgage, and to live in that house with no loan attached to it. The problem now is they're sitting on this bucket of money, so to speak, and the equity is just there not doing anything for them, not working for them. Now, we have a large percentage of our senior population that are homeowners. We also know that survey after survey has indicated that these folks want to stay in their home as long as they can. They don't want to go into assistant living facilities, by and large, and they definitely don't want to go into nursing homes until and unless it is absolutely necessary. Many a reverse mortgage client has commented to me, "They are going to have to take me out of here in a pine box." These factors combined have made almost the perfect storm of an environment for the reverse mortgage product. That, coupled with the education and the awareness on the part of the public about reverse mortgages, has fueled the growth along with the many safeguards that are built into the programs now. Recently, I read a report that indicates we have probably only penetrated the reverse mortgage market about 1½ percent of its potential.

Only 1½ percent of its potential?

So, we have only just begun. This thing is going to grow like crazy.

Definitely. There is plenty of business to be had in this niche. One important question is what types of reverse mortgages are available out there for people?

Well, that's another great recent change in the reverse mortgage world. Along with the awareness comes the consumer, the seniors, saying "I'm looking for this, I really want that, I'm looking for a program that offers such and such," so the market is driving the variation on existing programs and the creation of new programs. There are several options available today that weren't around maybe even a year ago, so this program is rapidly evolving, which is great news for the consumer and great news for the originator because we can now offer our senior citizen borrowers even more choices that can better meet their needs.

By and far, still the most popular reverse mortgage program is the FHA insured HECM, Home Equity Conversion Mortgage, you'll hear it referred to as the HECM. That is accounting for almost 90 percent of the reverse mortgage business that we're seeing done in our country today. It affords several safeguards that are important to the consumer. Number one is that it insured by FHA. To this current generation of seniors, the fact that the government backs something is very important. They see that as a real benefit. Even within the HECM itself, there are now several different variations, several different margins. Depending on the needs of the customer, the loan officer can tailor that loan to suit them. How much money do they need? What do they plan to do with it? How long do they plan to be in the home? All these things can be tailored to the borrowers' specific needs.

The next program that's available is the Fannie Mae Home Keeper®, which is the conventional arm of the reverse mortgage. The same safeguards built into the FHA HECM are a part of the Home Keeper®. However, the Fannie Mae product carries one added feature in that it can be used for the purchase of a home. So, let's say that a senior couple needs to sell their large, high-maintenance home that they've lived in for years and years, but, as we know, seniors want to remain homeowners, they don't want to go to assisted living or a nursing home, they would like to purchase a condo. They could take some of the proceeds from the purchase of their older, high-maintenance home, purchase a new condo or some other property that better meets their needs, and if they need to make up the difference, if there's a deficit, they can take out a Fannie Mae Home Keeper® Purchase Money Reverse Mortgage and move into that new property. They now have a home that better meets their needs and never have a mortgage payment. So, the Fannie Mae Home Keeper® fills a significant need for our senior borrowers.

The last type of reverse mortgage that is available today is the Jumbo Reverse. There are several variations of this program as each lender has built in its own features. Once again, carrying many of the safeguards that our senior clients have come to expect, the Jumbo Reverse Mortgages are tailored to homes valued in the million-dollar range and up. Therefore, even your senior homeowners with the higher value properties can use reverse mortgages to meet their needs or to meet their financial goals. Quite often, these homeowners with these higher value properties have some particular financial goals in mind and the reverse mortgage can be the perfect tool. I see the Jumbo Reverse as one segment of the reverse mortgage program overall that's probably going to continue to grow in popularity.

On these reverse mortgages, are there any requirements regarding age, income or anything else?

That's a great question. Let's talk about that for a minute. On a reverse mortgage, everybody on the deed must be at least age 62 at the time that the reverse mortgage is done. That is across the board. At this time, there is no way to get around that age requirement. Minimum 62. That's it. But since there is no repayment expected on the reverse mortgage, completely opposite of when you're qualifying for a forward mortgage, there are no income requirements. There are no credit requirements because, once again, there is no repayment. We've even been able to help people who have experienced a bankruptcy.

Can you imagine how stressful it would be for a senior citizen in a bankruptcy or foreclosure situation? I've just recently seen an article talking about the fact that bankruptcy among senior citizens is way up. Once again, further evidence that for those either living on a fixed income or those with rising expenses, their income is just not able to meet their needs. It's so easy for the senior to qualify for a reverse mortgage, that once you know the mechanics of the loan and how to communicate to the senior borrower, you'll wonder why you didn't jump into this niche sooner.

It is the complete opposite of what mortgage brokers are used to.

It truly is a mortgage in reverse if you think about it. Think about everything you know about a mortgage, throw it out, and start all over again.

Definitely; for mortgage brokers it goes back to the concept of learning and relearning.

That's exactly right.

The loan is opposite, so I imagine the marketing is opposite. What different types of things do you do to market reverse mortgages to make this easier for you?

That's right. Marketing reverse mortgages is quite different from marketing regular or forward mortgages, as we call them. Somebody told me that we reverse people made up that term, forward loan; I'm not sure, but maybe. You do several things differently. One of the biggest things that I found in my kind of trial-by-fire of learning is how you communicate with the senior borrower. In all of the marketing that we do, it's paramount that you understand that you're communicating with a senior and that's a mini study in marketing in and of itself because the senior population relates differently than any of your forward loan customers. Number one, there is the fear that they're being scammed;

that when something sounds too good to be true, it probably is. Putting out a clear and concise message is probably one of the most important things that you want to do when you're communicating with your seniors. I learned a valuable lesson when I was doing a seminar a number of years ago at a senior center.

One requirement for a reverse mortgage is that during the course of the loan, the borrower has to complete reverse mortgage counseling. We use the term 'counseling' all the time. You have first-time homebuyer counseling, certain programs have their own requirements for borrower counseling, etc. Well, in my presentation at the senior center, I kept using the word counseling referring to reverse mortgages until one woman in the audience got this weird look on her face. I said, "Ma'am, you look like you have a question, is there something I can answer for you?" She said, "Do you mean I have to go to a psychiatrist?" That is what counseling meant to her. Huge, huge lesson for me. I don't say counseling anymore. I've changed my presentation and I now call it an education session. It made me think, if she was the only one who spoke up, how many other people in the audience were thinking the same thing?

When marketing to our seniors, we need to completely remove jargon and, frankly, they're not impressed that we know a bunch of mortgage terms. They could care less. If you speak to them in concise, clear language, you will come across as professional and knowledgeable. Keep your messages simple, emphasizing the benefits of the loan. That may sound like Sales 101 to many loan officers, but it's often the little things that trip us up.

To receive your $247 in free bonuses: www.TheInsiderSecretsGift.com

There are so many ways to market the reverse mortgage product. Of course, in this format we only have time to touch on a few. I rely heavily on radio. I have found through my research and trial and error that radio will work well, but it has to be done a certain way in a certain format. It's much more than just running an ad. Direct mail marketing can produce good results as well. Once again, it has to be targeted, you have to know what you're doing, and probably one of the most important points with direct mail marketing is the concise, clear message. No jargon whatsoever, emphasizing the benefits. Obviously, as with any direct mail marketing, it's a commitment. You have to keep at it.

In addition, networking is a good way to get quality reverse mortgage leads and I always want to emphasize that people who are interested in originating reverse mortgages need to put themselves out there as the experts. Learn everything that you can about the program, which is what I did when I was starting out, and you'll be viewed as the expert and the person the seniors want to talk to. Your networking, like other marketing initiatives, must be targeted. You want to network with other professionals in senior-oriented businesses. I'll throw out just a couple of specific examples.

Elder law attorneys are a great resource for reverse mortgage leads. They are working with the target customer. They're working directly with the senior citizen and often, the family. When their attorney tells them to talk to you, they are pre-sold. They're not going to question the closing costs; they're not going to question the origination fee; their attorney told them to come to you.

That's a huge reference for you.

Yes.

Having a pre-sold client makes a mortgage broker's life so much easier. It is great to be able to help somebody without being questioned about rates and fees.

Yes. I think you'll find that when you're out there positioned as the expert in the niche, the fees objection is just gone. If the elder law attorney tells them to call you, they're calling you and it's when can you meet with me, when can we do this loan, when can we close? The discussion of the fees is right out the door because you're viewed as the problem solver, you're the one who's been called in to help them. Another great source of reverse mortgage leads is people who were my former competition when I was doing A paper loans. Since I have positioned myself as the reverse mortgage expert in my local area, the loan originators who used to compete with me now send me the seniors they cannot help. That referral is pre-sold on using me for their reverse mortgage. However, this all works because I use the system.

You're going out and using all of these different networking opportunities to bring business in and that has to make it easy. Jessika Ondrick mentioned how 80 percent of her business is just straight referral business, as opposed to doing direct marketing and some other things. How does your referral business, as you created the network, work for you?

I am probably in just about the same category as Jessika in that regard. The vast majority of my business right now is coming from referrals, other professionals and my previous clients. Senior citizens are a terrific source of referrals and, once you have done a good job for a senior client, they are going to tell everybody they know. Because the reverse mortgage of years and years ago used to be the product of the destitute, people were embarrassed if they had a reverse mortgage, but that's no longer the case. People are excited about it and, if you do a good job for the senior and their family, they are going to tell everybody that they know. It's nice to be able to have a good portion of the business coming from those personal referrals.

I don't think many mortgage brokers look at past clients as a great referral source.

That's absolutely correct. Part of the Reverse Mortgage Success System is the follow up of your previous senior clients because they are a gold mine, I think even more so than any other segment of the mortgage business. It really is a relationship business, not a transaction business. People jump in and jump out of the business because they may have been ignoring a great source of future business, which is their current client database.

Yes. There are so many things out there that we can do to stay in front of past clients.

Right.

Do you find it being a challenge dealing with some senior citizens and elderly people with much of our business being technology driven?

Actually, I don't. First, the senior citizen population is just terrific to work with. They are the most appreciative customers. They are incredibly respectful of your time. They do not expect me to work on evenings and weekends because they view that as family time, so Friday evening when you're out with friends or with your family, your phone is not going to ring. A senior citizen client is not calling you saying can you quickly run over and pre-qualify me for a reverse mortgage? That's just not how their generation views conducting business. Much of my business, personally, is done face-to-face. That's just how I started out doing it and that's how it's remained. That works for me and I have very little, if any, fallout. However, seniors are much more Internet savvy than we give them credit for. They may not have a computer in their home, but if they don't, I can almost guarantee you they are getting online either at the local senior center because many of them offer computer classes or they're going to the library and getting on the Internet there. There are some real opportunities to do some great Internet marketing, and I do rely on my website for lead generation.

We're working on an entire system as part of the Reverse Mortgage Success System to do online marketing in a strategic way to our senior clients because they are out there looking for information and they're using the Internet to do it.

So the Internet is a great way to reach potential clients. This is one of the most intriguing niches that I have learned about, which you have evolved into with some guidance of others. You mentioned Brian Sacks being somebody who definitely helped and coached you. How have mentors and coaches really helped guide you to be where you're at today?

That's a great question. I have been so fortunate to be able to work with some top-notch people in the business. I've learned that people who are truly successful, and I mean not only successful income-wise, but in the way they conduct business and in the way they conduct themselves, those types of people truly are willing to reach out and help others. Part of their makeup is that they're happy to help mentor people and, not only mentor them, but hold them accountable, which is part of it. It's great to say I want to do this, but along the way, you need somebody to hold you accountable and make sure that you're doing what you said you were going to do to get you there. I always encourage people to look around at the other people who are in your business or even a similar business, and approach them. Tell them you are looking for somebody to help with some specific things or to be a mentor overall and follow what that person does. Oftentimes, I find, from my own experience, these people lead by example, so watching what they're doing and learning from that experience makes a tremendous difference. The best learning experiences I have had came from what I call shadowing your mentor and learning from what they do.

Having business coaches has helped me tremendously in the last year. It's great to work closely with like-minded people who want to see you reach your fullest potential.

Right. Very much so. You can be part of a formal coaching program where somebody is really holding your feet to the fire in conjunction with surrounding yourself with like-minded people. Kind of a mastermind group. Coaching groups can be the force that drives someone to the next level of production because in a coaching group you are, just by the structure, interacting with others with similar goals.

You're challenged to implement as opposed to talk. They are there to support you, but only if you support yourself.

Absolutely correct.

How do you foresee the industry going as a whole, not just in reference to reverse mortgages, but the industry as a whole?

I see several things. First, obviously, the reverse mortgages hold an amazing amount of opportunity simply because of the aging population and the fact that once the baby boomers start to hit retirement age, there is going to be an unprecedented demand for reverse mortgages as well as other financial vehicles. I expect that we'll probably see some further variations of other mortgage products that might be similar to the reverse mortgage, also meeting the needs of the aging population.

One thing that I see happening industry-wide that I have been in favor of and actually pushing for, for years, is the licensing of the loan officers. I don't know if any of the other folks that you've spoken with have raised that issue, but if you think about it, we're the ones who hold the money in the transaction and, in many states, we're the only ones who aren't licensed. Go figure that one out. For example, in Maryland, as of January of this year, a substantial number of loan originators—there were some exceptions—had to be licensed. I think it raises our level of professionalism. I think it speaks volumes to the consumer about what we do and I think that as the consumer gets more and more savvy and more and more educated, they're going to look for mortgage professionals who are more educated. I think also that the niche products, people being a specialist as opposed to a generalist, I see that being embraced among originators. You know, going after those niche products and becoming the specialists and hitting that target market as opposed to trying to be all things to all people.

I think that's touching on a few of those things that you just said. One, being educated and having to be licensed. Two, becoming a specialist. I believe that will eliminate much of the bad publicity we get from the people that get into this business to make a quick buck.

Absolutely. If we're not licensed and anybody can jump in anytime there's a refi boom and jump out when it dries up, what does that make the rest of us look like? But that's what the public remembers.

There is no question that this business has its cycles of ups and downs. What kinds of things did you do to keep yourself focused during your 20-plus years in the business?

I've been in the mortgage business for about 20 years, including my taking applications and processing and then moving into origination. You've hit a couple of important points there, which I hadn't thought of it in this particular way, but shielding yourself against the bad markets is crucial. One significant benefit to being a specialist is you're not subject to the whims of the market. You're originating within your specialty, your education level is raised in that specialty, and you have systems in place so that no matter what the market does, your business is going to keep going. There are ups and downs everywhere, but you want to keep your business as consistent as you can. Both systems and positioning as the expert allows you to do that and take away that kind of roller coaster fear that people have. I think that is what drives many people who could be good originators out of the market—the burnout from the roller coaster ride. If they had a system in place, they knew that they were becoming the expert in their chosen niche, that fear is gone.

One more point to emphasize is the constant learning. For any of these mortgage products, no matter what they are and no matter what someone picks as their niche, ongoing education is necessary. I read everything I can get my hands on since reverse mortgages are changing at a rapid pace. Newspapers, trade publications, and many books are in my office. Being on top of your game and educated on your product will set the expert apart from the average originator. That, in combination with the systems, will help you weather the slightly slower market sometimes.

You have devised a system to help loan officers that can quickly and easily profit, especially from what we've been talking about today in reverse mortgages. What can people do to find out more about your product to create themselves as a specialist instead of a generalist?

When I was devising this system, I stepped back and thought about what I wish I had when I started. I backtracked and looked at all the things that I did wrong, because I did many things wrong. It was truly trial-by-fire for me and I worked to make it as easy as possible for someone to literally just pick up the system, run with it, and be originating reverse mortgages right away. The easiest way to learn more is to sign up for my free seven-part mini course, which is offered on my website. It's www.ReverseMortgageSuccess.com/isb. Easy to remember. Get a little taste of what reverse mortgages are all about and the potential to build your business working with the senior population.

I am in overload with great information right now. I used to be a generalist, not knowing that I was trying to be everything to everybody and then I realized that we are experts in this

business and we just need to position ourselves in that way. It has completely changed my career and life.

I'm sure your office has seen the benefits of that and what you say is true for most of us. When you learn the business, that's how you learn. You're a generalist. You learn all the different products, you try to keep all that information current, but when you realize that, just like so many other professions, the real way to go is to pick the niche that you have the most interest in and really become the local expert at it.

I'll share with you one quick story about one of our reverse mortgage success members in Texas. This person was completely unprepared for the onslaught of leads that he was going to get. He did some local marketing in his area in Texas and the leads were coming in so fast and he was writing so much reverse mortgage business in a short amount of time, that he actually had to hire another full-time loan officer just to handle the business that was coming in.

That is the best problem to have.

Sure. He saw what it was like to be the expert. There was no one else doing reverse mortgages in his area. So he had the whole local area all wrapped up.

I'm sure there are people who may understand reverse mortgages, but there are not many people who probably understand it as fully as your system lays it out.

Right. To be the expert, you need to have a full understanding of the product and the marketing that goes into it. They might have smattering of knowledge, they've heard this and heard that, but to really be successful at it, you want to be able to put yourself out there as the expert and have all the resources and tools at your hand. That's exactly what we do with the system—the physical system combined with the website. We post the resources and other tools on the Members Only section of the website because things are constantly changing and you need to be as up-to-date as you can.

Then you think, like you said earlier, with the marketing, there is trial and error that you've gone through, so why waste that extra money when you can invest in something that already has a proven track record?

I would say that one thing to people. Please don't waste the amount of money and the amount of time that I did. There's no need to do that. One question that I often hear from people who are concerned, especially with the downturn in some of the areas of the mortgage business, they don't have a big marketing budget right now. That's not a problem because, in my system, we talk about things that cost you literally nothing that you can do to market reverse mortgages. I always tell loan officers, don't let the fact that you don't have a marketing budget the size of Montana dissuade you from jumping into this.

There are many things in marketing that we do that cost money and there is stuff that you can do that doesn't, which is great because you can always do the stuff that brings in the business. Then, when you create revenue, you can do some of the things that are a little more costly but can also drive great revenues.

Absolutely.

As parting words, what words of advice would you give our readers?

To receive your $247 in free bonuses: www.TheInsiderSecretsGift.com

To be successful in the market the way we see things changing, my advice is to pick a niche, find some area of the market that is of interest to you, study it, learn everything you possibly can about it, become the local expert, and then position yourself as the local expert. You will be amazed at how your production will skyrocket and your income as well, because when you're perceived as the expert, as we've said before, rates and fees aren't an issue. People seek out experts all the time and seldom is the price even a consideration. Just take your originations to a new level and be in control of your business and in charge of your time as well.

Thank you. Time is a huge struggle that mortgage brokers have. Being an expert eliminates the 60-80 hour weeks. You can work 25 to 30 hours a week and have larger incomes and more personal time and family time, which you would think would be appealing to everybody.

Yes. Yes. Exactly right. That's another reason we have burnout is people are working so many hours and they just don't realize that when you're the expert in the niche, that's just not necessary.

Chapter Nine

Interview with Ken Schreiber

Ken Schreiber has eliminated cold-calling in his business and created a process that brings him a ton of borrowers that are sold on using him before he even talks to them. He is more than a mortgage broker to his clients; he is a financial planner who uses mortgage planning as his tool. Ken has created a high six-figure income with him and one processor, while working less than 30 hours a week.

Welcome and please give our readers some insight on your experience and background.

Thanks for having me, first of all. My niche in the mortgage industry is working with the credit challenged homeowners. I think it's important to tell you why that's my niche in the first place. In my early 20s, I went through a significant period of debt and credit problems myself and when I emerged from these credit issues personally, I realized that many customers of mine were asking, "How do I break this pattern of debt and credit issues? How do I finally get back on my feet and get normal loans like everybody else seems to be getting?"

I would regurgitate everything that I had done to become in debt and really in hopelessness. Then I would describe the steps to put myself back on the path to being credit worthy, getting the best rates and terms and subsequently being able to accumulate wealth from that point forward. I decided to focus on a niche that I was familiar with, having the experience, and just work with people to get from what I call "the ashes of debt and despair" to the heights of wealth building. The interesting thing about this market is it's continually growing with the high incidents of bankruptcies and delinquencies on mortgage payments and foreclosures. This niche continues to grow and if we position ourselves unique to everybody else, we're always going to have an abundance of business going into the future.

Definitely. What do you do exactly that is unique?

Well, I've heard this experience from customers; my clients always describe their previous experiences with other mortgage brokers of being filled with pain and empty promises. Many mortgagers look at trying to solve a problem as it exists today and they give no regard as to how this affects the borrowers in the long term. I've simply inverted that process and I look at target first. Meaning, what is the ultimate goal? What does the borrower really want to achieve in the long term? Well, they want to be able to save money. They want to be certain about their financial future; they want to be able to put their kids through school. They want to be able to save for retirement and possibly care for their parents in the event that they get sick. They want to be able to have adequate health care and tax saving strategies. All the things that don't seem obvious to the mortgage transaction are really what our customers want. So I look at what their end goal is and then back our planning back to today's date and figure out a plan from there rather than try to fix a current situation with no regard for future planning.

So you're more than just a mortgage broker to your clients.

I think of myself as a financial planner, where my tool is mortgage planning. There are financial planners that are insurance experts and there are financial planners that are experts in the stock market. My expertise just happens to be in mortgage planning and using the big picture as our blueprint for how we do things.

There have been many changes in the industry as of late and you have a unique system, so how is it still profitable?

Well, the customer's needs haven't changed. They're where I think a lot originated, especially with the chaos; the industry is missing that the consumer's needs are the same, in fact, they're growing. Right now, we have an opportunity—if you're positioned properly in the industry to really grab a tremendous amount of market share—because you're not competing against every Tom, Dick and Harry who entered the business when the refinance boom was going on. I think there is a tremendous opportunity for us to go out, make a huge statement for what it is that we do that's unique and really position ourselves for the next wave of refinance where we'll come back even stronger than in this previous boom.

Definitely. How do you suggest people prepare themselves for the next go-around?

I think there is a tendency for mortgage originators, especially those that are not familiar with direct marketing, to fear the market changes and typically that translates into less marketing. They want to hold on to every dollar that they have and they decide that they want to stop their marketing efforts. My suggestion to everybody who's reading this is to really take an aggressive stance with their marketing and go out and market more. This is a great time to cast a wide net and just grow a tremendous amount of inbound business by doing emotional direct response marketing.

What's interesting is I've been through this wave; I think this is my third time that I've been through this wave of chaos in the industry. In the previous two go-arounds I've witnessed that most companies decide they want to expand when the business and the market is at its height. What that invariably does is put you in a position where if the market changes you're really screwed. You have to contract and oftentimes that means total business failure. I suggest that most business owners go out and try to expand their operations now when the market is in chaos because when the go-around comes the next time, you're already going to be positioned for massive profits when the business starts pulling in even easier than it is today.

How are you going about finding this group of prospects?

The interesting thing about this group is these prospects come from so many different sources. We already mentioned that I work with borrowers who have had a bankruptcy that are trying to buy a house. That would be your post-Chapter 7 bankruptcy homebuyers. I actually have four tiers or four avenues for my niche, which is the Chapter 7 purchase market.

I have the Chapter 13 buyout market, which is a huge niche, especially in light of the new bankruptcy laws. I also work with credit-challenged homebuyers in subprime loans, trying to move them into either FHA or Conventional A market loans. Then my fourth component is working with borrowers that need debt consolidation to position themselves to get into the A market loan. Therefore, the market is huge and there are many more avenues than what I've just described. You have divorcees, you have borrowers who are self-employed with credit challenges. There are many, many niches and more niches are being developed every day that fall under the umbrella of the credit-challenged homebuyer.

As far as locating these borrowers, it's rather easy, because most of these borrowers can fall under readily available marketing lists, either through a data provider or through an industry publication or anything along those lines. So accessing this group of prospects is rather easy. One avenue that has always worked very well for me, which is actually a system that I've developed, is driving everybody into a teleseminar that has a common need or a common goal and letting the teleseminar do all the heavy lifting for me. You can find out more by visiting www.teleclassriches.com.

That's a different way of doing it. You're the first person that I've met that does things this way. How do you find that this increases your business and has clients already knocking down your door?

Let's go back to the beginning. When I started mastering the art of using emotional direct response marketing, my phone started ringing off the hook, which was a problem that I didn't have before I started marketing and I was struggling to find business. Once I understood how to get people to call me ready to do business with me, it actually caused another problem because I'm a one-man shop. It's just me and a processor and that's it. I would get a tremendous amount of unbalanced phone calls and I just couldn't manage it all. It was taking me 20 to 30 hours a week just to sift through the leads to find out who was a viable candidate for the services that I was offering.

Often, I wouldn't even be able to get through the entire list of people and it became frustrating because I was in the business not only to make a great living, but also to do it easily and liberate my time. I thought to myself, I want to talk to all these people because I feel that they want to hear the inflection in my voice. They want to hear the passion in what I do and how I convey it. So how can I do this? How can I accomplish all this as one person? All of a sudden, it just popped into my head, "Why don't you use a teleseminar? Why don't you bring the conversation to your customers where they are at their leisure so they can hear the message; let a recording do all the work for you. I started implementing the teleseminars as part of my lead generation strategy to really sift through all the people that I couldn't help and only get to the people that I could help so that my hours are spent in what I call green time or closing time.

That's where you're actually making more money.

Right. Most originators, if they were to look at their time, would find they spend the majority of their workweek on finding a prospect that they may possibly have a chance to work with. They spend the minority of their time on actually closing deals or networking with key people, key referral sources. I've simply used automation to invert that so my workweek is filled with just sitting with clients who are already sold on me, which includes my fees and my promise of service and networking with key referral sources. I spend my whole workweek on those activities that are highly efficient and profit producing. How this can be done can be found at www.teleclassriches.com.

How are you finding that your prospects respond to you and your message so well, why do you feel that is?

Because I'm one of them. My personal history, my history in terms of the struggle with debt and credit issues and a period of hopelessness and not knowing how to get ahead is something that I've lived and I'm free to tell that story to my customers, which I think really solidifies our relationship because I've been through it all. I've been through the collection process. I've been through the wage garnishment process. I've been through all the darkness that many of my clients are experiencing and as a result, we connect on a level that I think is a lot deeper than most loan officers can accomplish simply because of my personal history.

It's funny—I didn't come upon this niche intentionally. It just dawned on me, "Hey, why don't you do this?" Maybe sometimes I'm a slow learner, but I didn't discover how to focus in on this niche until about two years after I had been telling my story to clients. Repeatedly I would tell clients, "Listen, I've been where you're at. You'll get past this. Everything will be fine. This is what you have to do and I'll help you through the process." Then one night while lying in bed I suddenly thought to myself, "Why don't you just focus on this particular niche because all your clients are grateful, they're happy that you worked with them. They're not questioning your rates, points or fees." It's gratifying to work with people, to help them rise from the ashes of debt and despair. It just dawned on me, I'm just going to focus on this group, and that's when everything changed in my business.

That's huge too. I've noticed you get many loan officers out there that want to do everything.

Right, generally.

They want to be the subprime guy. They want to be the A paper guy. Often people don't even want to go towards the more difficult deal. You're saying that developing this niche has really honed in your skill and has allowed you to be more successful?

No question. I have a comment to make about the difficult loans. Some of the most profitable niches that exist really are the loans that are the most difficult to do and you hit it right on the head. Most loan officers want the easiest path to a commission check and some of the most difficult niches, some that I haven't even explored myself but I know there's a market for, are the ones that seem to be the most challenging because you just don't have any competition, you're the only person who would be doing it. These niches are emerging every day.

Lenders coming out with different programs allows you to create a different niche as well.

Correct.

You mentioned that you spend most of your time talking to your referral sources and doing that networking. Networking is actually a huge part of building a successful clientele as well. You have your direct marketing, but there are plenty of referral sources out there that people don't tap into. How has that changed things for you?

To receive your $247 in free bonuses: www.TheInsiderSecretsGift.com

I have a little bit of a confession to make about referral sources. I have been in the business since 1993 and for the first 10 years of my business, I really did not have any solid referral sources. I was doing everything on my own. Going out and finding business on my own, direct to consumer. Part of the reason for that, truth be told, is because I knew that I was a commodity to some degree. I knew that a referral source was looking at me and realizing, "Oh yeah, what's really different about what it is that you do?"

Having that fact in my mind discouraged me from going out and trying to locate referral sources. I realized that if I could find the key to what referral sources really, really want and fill that need then I would have a truly mutually beneficial relationship with every referral source that I have. The tool that I used to be able to do that is my knowledge of how to conduct profit-producing teleseminars. My clients have needs that extend beyond my expertise. However, to show my clients how valuable I can be for them, I have nationally recognized experts in various financial positions to provide free, quality advice. My clients appreciate the access to quality advice they never would have had access to and my referral sources get free publicity and marketing.

I realized that I had a system that would be able to give a parade of customers to handpicked referral sources. It wasn't just based on one transaction; it was an actual process that could guarantee a stream of income to all of my affiliates or all my referral partners. That was the difference because you can refer a transaction to a referral source, but the reality of the situation is they know it's a transaction and there's no solid relationship when it's just a single transaction. If you can show that you can give them an ongoing income stream, then your relationship is really solid. I've also taken my knowledge of how to use teleseminars in my business and I've simply taught all of my referral partners how to do the exact same thing in their business to not only increase their profits, but liberate their time, which just happens to suit everybody's needs and wants.

So you have a support team, more of a power team per se, that you work closely with?

Yes.

Working together, you are all able to generate business for each other?

Correct.

How do you find the key members within your team?

Because I'm working with credit-challenged buyers and I'm trying to help them build wealth, I'm looking at my wealth building team, which would be tax preparers, accountants, financial planners, CFPs, and real estate investor advisors. We have about a dozen different referral sources per area that I work with because I want to keep everybody tied to the geographic location. Anybody who could cater to the wealth building of my clients would be a viable candidate for partnership with us.

Obviously many people out there can be a part of that wealth building team. Another key or consistency to the most successful people in the industry is they work less and make more. It seems like a conflicting concept, so can you explain further on that?

Absolutely. If you have a specific niche that you work in and you are the expert of a niche and you have an expert process or you have a proposition that differentiates yourself from the masses then you, just by virtue of that distinction, are able to charge more for your services. It's the opposite of what most originators think. I have learned over time that it is one thing to be able to charge more, but more important is to substantiate that value in what you do. Because I take a position of building massive value with my clients, I know that my selling proposition is so unique that I have no problem charging the maximum fees for my service.

Interestingly enough, my clients, when they see the big picture and the value proposition, will make the same determination that I'm worth everything that I charge based on everything that I'm providing them pre and post-closing of their loan. I'll get back to the closing fewer loans. If you are charging appropriately for your services and once again, value being the key distinction, then it takes fewer loans to be able to make the same money than you would if you were simply average or a typical loan officer. Therefore, when they talk about making more money while working less, it's really about pricing yourself appropriately for each transaction.

Doing fewer loans as well, like you said with pricing appropriately, is a huge problem that many loan officers run into and I think it's a challenge for them to figure this out and say, "All right, when do I move on to the next deal? When do I move on if I have someone that I'm just unable to help?" How soon do you recommend that somebody move on to the next deal?

I've used teleseminars to assist me in this process. If you're getting an abundance of leads or people who are announcing interest in your products or services, there's an obligation to provide that borrower with the reality of the situation as quickly as possible. So if you're looking at a client and you know that there's just not any way that you're going to be able to help them in the short term, I've created a back-end process to help them help themselves over a short period.

It's all about setting the expectation at the very beginning. Because of what I do and the time sensitive nature of what I do, I can only take a limited amount of clients per month. I'm limited just because it takes time to prep everybody to get into a loan in the short term. All of my clients and prospects know that immediately. Many of my clients know that they're not ready to go yet. They're not in a position to close in the next 30 or 45 days, but they're looking for somebody to guide them and give them the path of how to get approved. That's really what they're looking for.

We've developed a process to walk them through that path and do it in an automated fashion so it doesn't take up all of my time. Essentially, it's a series of teleseminars teaching them exactly what they need to do to get approvable in a guaranteed period.

So your system is almost a four-part system.

That's correct.

It looks like you're bringing in four different parts. You have to have different messages, I would imagine, for those parts. So how do you manage or what is your key to building a massive appeal to your message?

One thing is just being sensitive to what the prospects are saying. Being a good listener. When I first started developing my series of teleseminars and really was the post-closing sequence of teleseminars, I was asking my clients what other goods and services they would need or want to be able to accumulate wealth and get out of this cycle of debt and despair. It was a matter of just asking the questions and then finding the answers for what they told me. It's as simple as that, but I think many originators, many salespeople in general, missed that. They're selling a client thinking they know what the client's needs are without really taking the small step of asking what the client's needs are.

As opposed to telling them?

Right. Most salespeople will try to sell without knowing exactly what the true motivation of the client is. So simply by asking the client, "What is your goal? What do you envision you would need to be able to get to the level of credit and savings that you're looking for?" What are those types of things? They would essentially give me the answers and it was my job just to fill that void.

You've been in the business for a long time and you've mentioned a couple of things that took you a while to figure out. We're talking about the success, but it was not an easy road to reach the level you've reached. What are some of the major roadblocks or challenges you faced trying to get to where you are now?

The first thing was how to get the business in the door. For the first 10 years, I was marketing just like everybody else. I had a telemarketing team. I taught my telemarketing team how to speak to my customers or to my prospects. I always had a unique selling proposition, but my delivery method was all through a telemarketing team. We all know what happened with that. The "Do Not Call" list came out and essentially killed that overnight.

I had to find a better way to do things and that was when I was introduced to direct mail. Specifically, emotional direct response marketing. That was relatively easy for me because I was already teaching my telemarketers how to speak to the clients to gain interest. All I had to do was take that same verbiage, put it on paper, and send it to a targeted list. Suddenly my lead flow would come in, actually much greater than it did with the telemarketing team, because it was done in a leveraged way. You could send out a mail order to 10,000 people rather than having one telemarketer speak to six people within a couple of hours. It was just a better way of delivering the larger message.

That was the first challenge: how to get leads in the door. The second challenge was really how to manage them and take them from being a lead to a paying customer. Like most originators, we spend all of our time trying to find a qualified lead, trying to find a prospect, and we spend very little time motivating that prospect to become a paying customer. One day I was sitting in my office, I happened to be moving one of my file cabinets from one wall to the other wall, and I was looking through my drawer of dead files or deals that I didn't do. As I started going through these files I just started doing a quick calculation of how much one of these represented in lost commissions. It shocked me how much I had lost simply by losing contact with my prospects and I knew that it was just a matter of time before they walked down the street and went to a competitor.

At that moment, I focused all of my efforts on finding a better way to convert people and spending less time on trying to find the better way to get people to raise their hand, which was already solved. I just had to find a better way to take them from being an interested prospect into a paying customer. That was the second challenge but it made all the difference in the world.

To receive your $247 in free bonuses: www.TheInsiderSecretsGift.com

Once you figured that out, did it start making your life easier and more successful?

Yes. If you have a system that works and you're getting leads coming in the door, then that isn't the problem. You need to spend your time and efforts on the money that's really made, which is converting clients into paying customers and then protecting those clients from competition forever.

The last would be networking and that's where all of our time and effort should be focused as originators because that's where all of our profits are made or lost.

It's tough that you see many people in the industry who close that deal and then after that there's no other point of contact. It amazes me.

It's such a limited thinking because you have no idea what the customer's needs are, what's going in their private life. To assume that they have a good rate, they won't want to refinance or they won't want to take money out for some purpose is really limited thinking because you're making the assumption that you know everything about their circumstances. That simply isn't true. We focus on thinking outside of the box and filling our clients' true needs, which are in my niche, "How to accumulate wealth, how to get back on their feet, how to not struggle with debt." There are so many other avenues that they have that are in need that might not directly translate into a loan for you, but you have to believe that it translates into referrals and it also creates networking opportunities with your affiliate partners.

After you have a client and you're done taking care of them on that one specific transaction and you've helped them get involved with your wealth building management team, how many

times do you touch that client after that? What types of things are you doing that separate you from other people?

My contact management with clients that I've done loans for is two times per month via newsletter and teleseminar. I send out a newsletter every month and the focus of the newsletter is really trying to maintain that relationship with the client. This is not a sales newsletter, it's a relationship newsletter. It's a newsletter designed to keep the relationship intact. It's all about them. It's all about services that I'm aware of that could help them build their wealth. Same with my teleseminar series. It's all about the client's needs.

I see newsletters getting bigger in all industries. How long ago did you start doing your own newsletter?

We created the newsletter about two and half years ago.

Is that a monthly piece you send out that talks about different aspects or is it tailored toward every client?

It's tailored to every client because it's not about a specific financial need. It's simply about the relationship that we have. Much of the content is, "Hey, I just noticed something that I thought would be interesting for you or somebody you know. Just wanted to drop you a quick note." It's really about the relationship and not about any specific financial topic; that's the key to it. Our business is a relationship business. It is not a transaction business and many originators miss that. They sell numbers. They sell programs, but they don't sell the relationship and the relationship is everything.

Definitely. Well, they want to have someone that they feel they can go to with any question as opposed to a loan officer or mortgage broker, but I'm sure you probably don't go and tell all your clients first that you're a loan officer.

Absolutely.

How do you position yourself, instead of saying you're a loan officer? What's something you do to position yourself with your clients to separate you?

I'm an expert in helping people resolve their debt issues and build wealth. That's my expertise. That's the selling proposition that I have with my clients: I'm an expert in helping them eliminate bad debt and rise from the ashes and build wealth, that's the proposition. Now the phrasing of it may differ depending on whom I'm speaking to, but the core concept is that. My vehicle or my tool is always mortgage lending. I'm very clear that that's my vocation, but I position myself with a bigger picture.

Looking at the bigger picture with the ups and downs of the mortgage business, how has your system allowed you to keep yourself focused on your ultimate goal?

The focus is on systematizing your lead-generation campaigns, I use pre-recorded teleseminars (www.teleclassriches.com) and then I focus on quickly converting pre-sold prospects into paying customers. When I decided to take my focus and shift it to converting prospects to clients, I eliminated the peaks and valleys in my business. I filled a steady stream of prospects that would close at various times throughout the year. In the mortgage industry, and you probably understand this, we suffer through grave months. Then if we have a great month, we're petrified because the next month isn't looking so good or the pipeline's empty. This is a big problem in our industry and it's really one of the easiest problems to fix. The way that I fixed it was really focusing on building my pipeline and managing the clients through a series of steps so that they would end up becoming a paying client over time and that solidified the way my business operated. It made my business predictable. It made my business consistent and it became much more profitable with that shift and focus.

How do you manage all those prospects and turning them into paying clients, while being a one-man show? Other companies have someone to answer the phones, someone to process the deal, someone to assist and all these different people in an office. How do you manage your business with a part-time processor and you?

As I mentioned before, I created mini-mes on teleseminars. I simply hired myself is the way I phrase it. I allow my recorded me to do much of the heavy lifting through a series of teleseminars. Prospecting for a new client is usually where all of your time is wasted. So I automated that process by driving every one of my interested prospects into teleseminars. In the series of teleseminars, I describe exactly what it is that I can do, whom I can help and whom I can't help, and let the systems filter out waste, if you will, or the people that I cannot help in the short term. The system really just spits out the people I can work with on a day in/day out basis.

It took my time from 40, 50, 60 hours to being closer to 10 to 15 hours each week, all in making these processes work. It's about leveraging your time through automation and knowing exactly what your goal is. A loan originator will really help you do this efficiently.

You have decided to take your system and clone it for others to use, so what's the best place for someone to learn more information about your system and working with you?

To receive your $247 in free bonuses: www.TheInsiderSecretsGift.com

To learn more, go to www.teleclassriches.com for information about my system and how to use teleseminars to skyrocket your profits. One thing to note is I was never interested in being a big shop. I always wanted to be a profitable shop and I think many originators, specifically the business owners, might confuse those concepts. By working with other larger firms, I witnessed that the business owners oftentimes were getting the lesser share of the profits; it was all going to the loan originators and to overhead. I wanted to switch things. I wanted to be in a small shop that had low overhead and high profits and that's what I developed. The only way you can do that is by having systems to do the work for you, which is what Teleclass Riches will provide.

That's fantastic. The most successful people in the industry do tons of readings. I think all people should be students of life and constantly try to learn. What are some of the top books that you've read that have really helped you zone in on what you've done in your life and helped you get where you are going?

I am a student of marketing. I read absolutely everything related to direct marketing and advertising; one big influence in my life is Dan Kennedy, for sure. I own everything that Dan Kennedy has ever written. I'm a student of Kennedy. I'm a student in the mortgage industry of loan officer success and Brian Sacks, who you had mentioned earlier. Brian happens to be my director mentor, so I spend a tremendous amount of time focusing on the psychology of selling and marketing. It's my passion. I have an endless curiosity and an endless thirst for knowledge when it relates to marketing. The most important part is actually taking your knowledge, testing it, and trying it yourself. You can never become a good marketer just by reading a book.

You actually have to experience it; you actually have to do things on your own and test the waters yourself. There's no better way to do it than just to jump in and try it. It's all a matter of testing and trying things. One thing I'd also like to mention about teleseminars. New niches are being developed every single day. I have used teleseminars to test how viable a new niche is because it's inexpensive and it has tremendous results when trying to find a new niche to focus on. Just a side note on the importance of teleseminars.

Great. People will hopefully go to your site and check this out because it's a unique product that can eliminate some of the grunt work and make your life as a loan officer more profitable and enjoyable. If you had to come up with some last advice to give as we near the end of the interview, what would you want to tell people?

I think in light of what's going on in the industry I just want to give everybody the assurance that this market, the business that we are in, the mortgage industry, is a great business to be in. If you focus your attention on marketing first and becoming a student of marketing then you will survive and thrive, no matter what the industry or the media says about the market, you will always be getting the lion's share of the profits. I guess the parting words I would give to everybody is simply just press on, market more and everything will solve itself. Don't be afraid.

Chapter Ten

Interview with Brian Sacks

Brian Sacks is a manager at Integrity Home Funding. He has done over 5900 loans for one billion in total production. Brian started as a realtor 23 years ago. He's been a banker, broker, loan manager, regional VP, and owned his own shop.

Brian is a national expert on working with bankrupt and credit-challenged buyers. He's trained thousands of loan officers around the world on how to close fewer loans, make more money, and have a life. He's the president of Mortgage Web Success and a chairman for NARLO. He's also a columnist for *Mortgage Originator, Mortgage Press, Broker Magazine*, and has spoken for many major companies.

Brian, I want to make sure that our readers fully understand everything you have done, so please go ahead and tell us a little more about your experience

I'll give you the *Readers Digest* version. I began as a realtor in the mid '80s. After a year being a realtor I became a loan officer, became a manager, regional Vice President at a national company, and eventually opened my own shop. Been a broker, been a banker, working for a bank.

Five years ago, I started a training company for loan officers called loanofficersuccess.com. I'm trying to teach originators around the country from my mistakes and give them the ability to close more loans, make more money, and actually have a life and time to enjoy it. I guess career wise I've closed about 5900 home loans at this point over 20 years. Close to a little over a billion dollars in production.

From that, obviously, there are many lessons; the big one I'll give you right now is pick a niche. Pick a niche, become an expert to that niche, and let everyone know about it. So from loanofficersuccess.com, we train thousands of loan officers around the country. Our newsletters, our coaching programs, a platinum plan—loan officers around the country actually come into mastermind summits for two days and work on each other's businesses. I also have a half hour consultation.

One frustration I quickly had was most techniques had been off-line techniques, marketing, and publicity. This was disturbing to me because I was technophobic and afraid of computers. Really didn't even have an e-mail address. After much struggle, I figured out how to leverage the Internet with follow-up generation while I was busy trying to get the bills out the door.

I built a system for myself and it became so successful that we now have hundreds of members using it around the country; it's called mortgagewebsuccess.com. You can find it at whatbrianuses.com. Lastly, one passion has always been getting to deal with the real scum of our industry.

Many people in our industry give us all a black eye. It's

hard for a consumer to distinguish between a good lender and a bad lender, especially when you have people giving misleading quotes or selling the wrong products or using false advertising in the paper, putting in rates that they don't have or never had. After you teach a certain level of success, it's time to give back to the industry.

Therefore I created an association with others around the country, and I guess what's different about the association is that it's built by loan officers for loan officers. Companies cannot even join.

We started the National Association of Responsible Loan Officers so that consumers could really distinguish the good guys from the bad, and also give loan officers around the country a forum and playing field for the originators, not just companies. Most originators would feel like the lone wolf out there. It is called NARLO and you can get more information at NARLO.com.

That's pretty much what I've done in the industry. There's more but I want to keep it brief.

Definitely. You have created a career in the mortgage industry for many years, so why did you decide to get involved over 20 years ago?

I want to say two more things now that I think of it and then I'll answer your question. I also wrote a book for consumers called *Yes You Can Get a Mortgage if You Had a Bankruptcy or Foreclosure* and I talked to ABC, NBC, Comcast, and radio stations around the country; I mention that because it's critical that everybody positions themselves as experts.

People should also realize—and this is worth writing down and taping to your computer—"It's all about who is chasing who." You always want to be in a situation where people are chasing you, and not you chasing them. I spent 15 of my 23 years chasing business, and had all sorts of creative ways to do that. I finally figured out that it's all about them chasing you.

To answer your question, I barely graduated high school. Had a little bit of college, a couple of semesters under my belt. I felt that college was not for me. It's right for some people, but not for me. So as far as selling real estate, I figured, why would I go back to college when I'm making more money than I would be in college? And I'm 20. So why would I do that?

So I poured all my effort into real estate. I was doing very well. I was working for Merrill Lynch Realty. It was in the mid '80s—I don't think they are around anymore. The original vice president of the company took a liking to me and saw my work ethic and my sales ability, and was just starting a mortgage company and asked me to join him. At 20 years old, sure, why not? Let's do that. I've been doing it ever since.

It is amazing to make that type of money at the age of 20. Many mortgage brokers are working long hours every day, especially in a tougher market. So what kind of advice do you have for our readers regarding working less and making more money?

I have to fix that statement. I say close more loans, make more money, and have a life. The reality that I practice in my own business is actually closing fewer loans, making more money per loan, so you can have a life. The reason I don't say it that way is that I don't think most people believe it.

We're programmed in our industry to try to be everything to everybody. So the first thing I would argue is that every loan officer find a niche ASAP. I call it a 30-second elevator speech. So if you choose what you do for a living, and you say you're a loan officer, right? My first question is, gee, you're a loan officer, what's your rate? We all hate rate shoppers, yet we feed right into the problem of rate shoppers by commoditizing ourselves.

If you were to ask me what I do for a living, I would tell you, "I help buyers who have had a bankruptcy or credit issue get into a home with very little down at attractive rates." Every industry has gotten this except ours. If you need an attorney, you don't generally go to a regular attorney because you need a divorce attorney, or a tax attorney, or a litigation attorney, or a real estate attorney, or a business attorney.

If you were to break your toe, would you go to a dentist? Of course not, but they're both doctors, right? If, God forbid, you had a stomach ulcer you wouldn't go to a gynecologist. Every industry has gotten that concept except for us.

The big idea to report is don't be a generalist; be a specialist. Specialists now are able to name their hours, and they're able to charge you appropriately for their services. Take a dentist, right? You go to a dentist and then you go to a surgeon, you have to pay more.

So you're saying one key is obviously to create a niche and become a specialist.

When you talk to someone that has a problem, it's now not about rates and points, you have to solve the problem. I'm able to do significantly fewer loans. Only a quarter of the loans, I used to do 30 to 40 loans a month. I now do 6 to 8, maybe in a very high month I do 10. But I'm earning 5 points for each one. So there is a big difference there.

I know it's going to create deals right now. I'm going to miss a deal. I can't afford it, this deal might go bad, blah, blah, blah. The reality is that 72 percent of my business is A credit buyers. The niche I have is 28 percent of my business. More important, last year 81 percent of my income came from that 28 percent of the business. That means that I can do 72 percent of my business and only lose 20 percent of my income, less than 20 percent.

There are a few who are wondering what niches are out there. We have reverse mortgages, that's the biggest niche to ever hit the marketplace. My former processor, who I worked with for many years, is now an expert teaching reverse mortgages and has done very well for herself. She put together a program called reversemortgagesuccess.com/isb. There are 5500 prospects every day. Seventy-five million Americans are already eligible for a reverse mortgage.

So that's one niche. You have a niche of buyers who are paid in cash, or don't show all their income, self-employed but doing well. Why not have a niche of working 5 percent down bid docs. There's a whole other niche of construction, rehab loans. There's a niche of buyers who have good credit, good income, but no cash. You can do 100 percent loans. Niches are endless.

It separates you from everyone else, it allows you to close fewer loans, have more money, have a life, and more importantly, not have to deal with rate shoppers.

Rate shoppers are definitely a hassle—they'll leave you for $100.

When people come to me, the question is not what your rate is; the question is are you for real when you settle.

You have mentioned a large group of niches off the top of your head, so where are some places our readers can go to find out more valuable information on niches?

It depends on the niche you want. This is what I deal with loanofficersuccess.com. I give you one site: reversemortgagesuccess.com/isb, where you should go if you want to do reverse mortgages. Then you'll want to generate the leads online and follow up with them automatically and realize how to truly have an online presence. It infuriates me because all the companies online right now are selling you a crappy brochure website that you can't even track. So you view it as a fax machine. Like it's a cost of doing business.

In reality, I get three or four deals a month, and many of our members are making tens of thousands each month from generating online leads and following up with them automatically. We all stick to follow up. I relate to whoever gets married on the first date. What we do as loan officers, mail one time to one person, and you never follow up.

Most people need 6, 7, 10 contacts before they do anything. So how great is it if you could automate that? That's what we do with the mortgagewebsuccess.com and findoutwhatbrianuses.com. I don't want this to be an infomercial for what I do, but give resources, tools, so people don't have to make the same mistakes I made for 17 years.

Can you touch on that a little bit more—about your automated system, your follow up, as well as generating leads using the Net.

Sure, there are a couple of points. The first point is what we really do in brand advertising, I call it being an advertising victim. All of us every day have people calling us, e-mailing us, faxing us, and mailing to us, their new hair-brained idea. Maybe it's a picture on a shopping cart, or a picture up at the supermarket, or a billboard on the street.

All these branding appeals are being sold to us by people who have never originated a loan, have no clue how to originate a loan, may not even own a home. They are going to be telling us how to generate business. Here's something for everybody to pay attention to: you need to make sure that every dollar you spend, every penny you spend, is trackable and accountable. So let's talk about that in terms of the website. If you have one of these crappy brochure websites, you may know how many people came to your site, but the thing you don't know, and the most important thing you don't know, is where they came from.

Did they come from a rental campaign in an apartment complex? Did they come from a homebuyer magazine? Did they come from a newsletter that you sent out, or a referral? How do you know where they came from? If you don't know where they came from, how do you know if your advertising's working? If you don't know if your advertising's working, why are you wasting precious money, especially in this market?

True, you have to know what's working and what's not so you can get your highest return on investment from your marketing.

Yes, everybody's complaining that they don't have money for marketing but they spend money on things that they can't track, or see if it's working or not. The next problem is that you know how many people came but you don't know who they are. So knowing that 1924 people came to my website last month doesn't help me if I don't know who those people are, and I can't follow up with them.

For the web there's something called auto responders. Auto responders are just pre-programmed e-mails. So when people come to my site they opt in, they get a free report, they give you permission to follow up with them, and then every couple of days for 90 days or 60 days, or however many days you want to program it for, they get an e-mail from us with another tip automatically while I'm sleeping.

See the real point here, and I don't want this to be lost on everyone, is a loan officer's dream. A loan officer's dream in my opinion is waking up in the morning, getting a phone call, and on the other line is a buyer who doesn't care about your rate, and is already sold on you. Would you agree?

I would definitely agree.

That's a dream, right?

Oh, every day.

That's my reality and the reality of many of my members. The reason it's a reality is this, have you ever seen the movie *Groundhog Day*?

Yes.

Okay, so in *Groundhog Day*, Bill Murray wakes up every day, and it's the same thing every day, over and over and over again. It's called *Groundhog Day*. I call it productionists. Most of us freak out when the phone is not ringing. Do you agree?

Yes.

I will tell you that all that happens when your phone rings is your neck hurts and you get grumpy. Because you're answering the same questions, think about it, all of us have the same rap that we give over and over and over again; would you agree with that?

I agree.

Okay, so you say the same thing repeatedly. Now if the phones are not ringing, you get upset. What I found, and it took me awhile to find it, to be fair, but I found that instead of having the phone ring, instead of saying the same thing repeatedly to people all day long, why don't I just say it in a free report? Why don't I give them my spiel, my rap, in a report.

The report just tells them who I am, why they should listen to me, what's going to happen to them, and testimonials of my expertise. They get it by calling an 800 number 24 hours a day, and having it mailed or faxed to them, or going to our website, which is what I prefer. On the website they opt in, they get my sales message, they read it, if they don't like it, they don't call me.

If they do like it, they call, and now they've already heard the sales pitch, or my rap, and they're already sold on using me. Now the deal is when can we meet. So this letter tells them exactly what's going to happen, exactly who should call, exactly who shouldn't call, exactly what they can expect, testimonials from past satisfied clients, and me handling all of their objections. Because most of the objections are the same ones over and over again.

So why not do it this way, it's so much easier. The question I am asked is, "Brian if you're such a hot shot, and you travel around the country, then how do you do business?

How can you be in Detroit last week speaking for *Mortgage Rich Native* magazine, giving seminars to 300 loan officers, and still do business?"

Well, I don't get that many calls. The calls I get are for people who are already sold on using me, and I don't need to do that many loans because every one loan I do probably equates to what many reading this will get if they did 10 deals, or 6 deals, depending on the part of the country. Therefore, I'm making more per deal, do fewer deals, and totally automated the whole process.

Many people out there aren't doing that, so it's a great thing to do. I've finally automated my system as well. It saves time, and you're not dealing with many of those tire kickers.

Right. I can't even imagine how I functioned. I used to function only by saying, "Gee, I need to get as many opportunities as I can." To be honest, that's backwards thinking.

You need to maximize the opportunities that you have, right?

Sure, absolutely.

What do you say to people that do ask you about rate, or people that you have sitting on the phone and questioning working with you?

I don't entertain talking to them.

Okay, it makes sense.

If somebody says to me, "We're looking for the lowest rate," I'll tell them, "I really appreciate that, I'm sure you drive a Hyundai, or a Yugo." They say, "Well how do you know that?" "Well, obviously you're always looking for the cheapest so I'm sure you wouldn't drive a nice car, because all cars cost different." But I'll educate them, and I'll tell them what to shop for, what to watch out for.

I'll tell them, "I'm sorry we can't do business but, I'm clearly not the lowest rate if that's what you're looking for." The real answer to your question is that I rarely get that call. The reason I rarely get that call is that people don't get to speak to me until they've heard my sales message.

Which is actually a good thing because like you said, you're giving your pitch on the front-end.

I may hear that question maybe once or twice a year.

This brings me to the question about creating longevity in this business. What are you using in your business to maximize your referral business and also keep the clients you have?

First of all, do a good job. Be honest. Be reputable. Really care about your clients. We have put together a survey at closing, asking for referrals, and rating ourselves. We don't care what the rating is, to be honest, we just want the referrals.

Here's the sneaky way to enforce the referral. I created a 4 x 6 card, a cardboard stock, they're four to a sheet, bound and stapled, and already perforated. A week after closing we send the buyer 15 to 20 We Just Moved cards with the buyer's name. It contains the buyer's name, new address, and at the bottom our company logo, my name, phone number, and website address, which is important.

They take this card and send it to all the people, friends, family, co-workers that they need to notify that they moved. They're sort of endorsing us. See how that works? I think the whole thing costs three dollars. Now the people they send it to keep it up on their refrigerator, and it has our information on it. So you can see Shirley sending it to her cousin Jody, and Jody going, "Oh, Brian Sacks, was he good? I've heard of him."

That's a great tip.

It's worth a million dollars. We also do a monthly newsletter. Do not send a beautiful monthly newsletter, glossy and so forth. The boring one that you know is a newsletter you toss in the trash. Ours is an 8- to 10-page newsletter. It's so successful we do it for our members. It has topics people care about. And it has direct response advice so it is passed around and bounced back.

How would someone go about becoming a member and utilizing that service?

It's all part of loanofficersuccess.com. You can get it there. It works because it's ugly. It works because it has contacts. It works because it's not just a recipe, and someone telling you what's happening in the mortgage market. In any marketing strategy, you have to answer the question, who cares. With those newsletters, truly no one cares.

That's true. They just get tossed to the side. It amazing how the uglier the marketing, the better its response.

Well, I don't mean to say it's hideous or anything. But it's clearly not the glossy reproduced four-page letter. It's an 8- to 10-page newsletter that we send in an envelope and it has interesting topics that are not mortgage related. It's sort of like an *Inquirer,* if you will. Each person you sell to is a previous client who already trusts you, knows you, and likes you. So if you're missing that opportunity, you're missing the big one.

To receive your $247 in free bonuses: www.TheInsiderSecretsGift.com

Another thing important to success is being involved in the industry in order to create creditability. What is a good organization to belong to?

That's NARLO, National Association of Responsible Loan Officers, and it's NARLO.com. If you went to a seminar on it that's NARLO.com/free. It's really a labor of love for me and something I'm proud of.

What is NARLO doing?

First, it has a monthly newsletter where we bring together all the experts, and give people the most current mortgage industry updates. Who wants to read all that, your eyeballs will fall out. Therefore, we try to give things that make everybody current. Each member has their own page on NARLO. So a consumer could come to the website, click on any of the states, and find the members closest to them. One other service we offer is really important. Consumers are looking for information, would you agree?

They're always looking for more info.

Basically, they're looking for information so they aren't screwed. They don't want to be taken advantage of. Most loan officers ignore that and hope that consumers just won't ask the question. That's a big mistake. At NARLO, we've put together a consumer brochure telling them the six mistakes to avoid when shopping for a mortgage.

It's written from a loan officer perspective, not HUD. See, HUD's brochure says call 20 loan officers, get 20 good faith estimates, here's what you're looking for. It discourages people from doing anything that we want them to do. We've come out with our own brochure and we encourage you to give it to your people. So now, imagine you have a prospect in your office and you're giving them a brochure telling the six mistakes to avoid when shopping for a mortgage. Do you think that gives you credibility?

It definitely does.

Plus we have our code of ethics that our members hang in their office. They have their membership certificate. We encourage them to put the NARLO logo on everything. We had one member send in a tattoo on themselves. They won the contest that month, obviously. But think about it. You tell somebody that you're a member of the National Association of Responsible Loan Officers and it has a lot of meaning. We teach our members how to use NARLO to get free publicity.

We give our members templates, various press releases, and a whole special report on how to get free PR. So now you go to your local real estate paper in town, or your local radio station, or TV station and say, we're at the peak of homebuyer season. There's so much predatory lending and fraud going on, and I'm a member of the National Association of Responsible Loan Officers. I'm wondering if your readers would like to know the six mistakes to avoid when shopping for a mortgage. Think you'll get some publicity?

You'll definitely get publicity on that.

Those are some examples. We have several programs that are geared for loan officers—again, we're built by loan officers for loan officers. All of the directors on our board are originators. We have a discount with many vendors for loan officers. There are many services that we would need as originators, not company owners, that all of our members can take advantage of like FedEx, or health insurance,

Staples, Office Depot. It's more than that; I could talk to you for an hour just about NARLO.

One service is a good thing that we do but it's a bad experience most people have. If you're in the business for any length of time, people will file a complaint against you. Doesn't matter if you're right, doesn't matter if you're wrong. And the consumer now has no idea where to go.

So where do they go? They go to an attorney and the attorney tells them to call the state or the bank commissioner. And the state comes and audits your entire office; you're guilty even if you're innocent. Therefore, we created a whole arbitration center so that a consumer can come to us and we can mediate the problem without needing to go to the local state or authority.

That's actually a huge benefit in helping to mediate a situation as opposed to dealing with the other avenue. NARLO is a great place to gain valuable information. What are some other good publications that our readers can pick up that will help them become better marketers and originators?

Well, I'm a huge Dan Kennedy fan. I've learned so much from Dan Kennedy and Bill Glazer. You could go to their site and actually take a three-month free trial of their newsletter, it's all about marketing.

I get that myself.

Sign up for the free success marketing strategies and every couple of days in your inbox you get another success marketing tip. I like *Think and Grow Rich*; the problem is you can't just think and grow rich because you will never get rich, you'll just be thinking a lot. But I do like a book called *Psycho Cybernetics* by Dr. Maxwell Maltz; I read and re-read it constantly. There's another good book called *Influence, The Psychology of Persuasion* by Robert Cialdini. I've read all of the Dan Kennedy *No BS* books. I think they are 10, 12 bucks on Amazon.

I read these types of books and the truth is, once you think you know everything, you're dead.

That's what I tell everyone—you'll never know enough in this business.

That's very good advice.

This seems like a lot of information and a lot to do for someone. What would you say to someone who is thinking about becoming better at their career?

Well, you have to believe it. Either you buy it or you don't. And if you don't, that's a condition of insanity—you're producing over and over again and expect something different to happen—that's insane. It was very scary for me when I made that transition. However, I will tell you for myself, for all of my members, it really changes your life.

If you work backwards buying the business, you shoot more needs instead of letting the business run you; you really can do it. As I told you, I didn't know this for 15 years. I made every mistake in the book. The good news is I learned. It's not that I'm smart. It's because I learned. "Gee, I hate this; I wonder if there is a better way to do it; let's try this." Most people would rather bitch about it and just tolerate it. I didn't want to do that anymore.

Dan Kennedy and Scott Tucker both say you have to take action.

To receive your $247 in free bonuses: www.TheInsiderSecretsGift.com

I have a great deal of respect for Scott and what he teaches, Scott is a doer. Scott is an implementer. I am a doer. I am an implementer. So you talk about it, or as I say, be about it. I think both Scott and I are about it. Scott's very successful, and truly leading the lifestyle, and nobody in the business would believe it because it's not the way you're supposed to do things.

The big key to success is to look around at what everyone else is doing and do the exact opposite, you'll be fine. I think Jim Rohn said that.

That's huge. I used to follow the rat race until I discovered these great mortgage marketers, such as you. They do separate themselves and it amazes me how, when I talk about this stuff to some people I know in the industry, they look at me as if I'm crazy.

Yes, they look at you as if you have three heads. The truth is I wouldn't push the issue, let them keep doing what they're doing.

That is fine with me.

When I tell people what I do, they look at me like, you can't do that, how do you do that? And I'm sure they say the same thing to Scott. The reality is you can do it, and not only can you, you need to. However, I also believe that most loan officers are one-trick ponies. They're all about taking the next idea and throwing it up against the wall before they've gotten the first one to work. If I were to give you a million dollars right now, and tell you to go to Kalamazoo, what's the first thing you would do? You have to be there by noon tomorrow. What's the first thing you're going to do?

I imagine go get a plane ticket.

Okay. The problem is there's no airport in Kalamazoo. Now what do you do?

Well, I guess I could drive but that's a long haul.

You could drive, right? But you don't remember where you're going. See, you're taking action right now. When I ask loan officers, this is exactly what they tell me, I'm going to go to training, I'm going to drive, I'm going to fly, I'm going to do all these things. In reality you don't even know where Kalamazoo is. So the first thing you need to get is what?

You need to get a map and figure out where it is.

You need a map. Exactly. Every originator out there does not have a map. They're just going to drive, fly, run, whatever. They don't have a map. So the first thing you need to do is get a map. I call that a goal worksheet. One of the first things you have in my system is a goal work sheet. Because how are you going to get anywhere if you don't have a map?

It's like a table; you need three or four marketing tools working for you consistently that you test each week and work on to have success. So if you have a table with one leg, it's going to collapse. Two legs, it's going to collapse. Three legs, it's wobbly. Four legs, it's sturdy. Does that make sense?

It makes very good sense.

Most loan officers don't get that. Most loan officers don't realize that. Most loan officers obviously don't practice that, they don't understand it.

That's definitely great advice. You stated earlier that this took about 15 years to take form, so what mistakes did you make before you finally figured out a system that works perfectly for you?

Well, there are about 12 of them. We don't have the time;

this would turn into a four-hour call. Being a generalist was probably the biggest mistake. Paying people to chase me—Scott doesn't use this, but every other guru in our industry, the big names, are teaching you creative ways to chase business. I'm not saying they're not successful ways, I'm just telling you that there are creative ways to chase business.

All of what I'm about and what I know of Scott, is fall back on the business chasing you. That's a big difference.

It's what you touched on earlier too; your clients come to you.

Right. They are already sold on me.

As we wrap up our conversation here, Brian, what's some important advice you would give to our readers as a fast action start list.

First, start with a goal sheet. Plan out what you want to get so that you can tell what's working and what isn't. Every month you should be writing loans you have, how much revenue you made, and where it came from. So let's say I wanted eight loans a month, and so my goal sheet might look like two deals from Realtors, two deals from direct mail, two deals from referrals, and two deals from online marketing. Now at the end of the month, I can look at my goal sheet; compare it with my actual to see if I reached it.

Another big thing, let me give you this idea, which I think is utterly disgusting and misleading. Ready? How do you judge the industry as a success? What would you call a loan officer's success?

A loan officer's success is due to their loan value.

To receive your $247 in free bonuses: www.TheInsiderSecretsGift.com

Right. You hit it right on the head. So you're judged by how many loans you produce, the buying of those loans. I can't tell you how many trophies I have in my office, and I look at them as my idiot trophies. Because they remind me how stupid I was. Closing 30, 40, 50 loans a month, not being with my family, ready for a nervous breakdown, tired, haggard, just ugly.

Now I close 8 to 10 loans a month and make more than I ever did closing 20 or 30. The whole industry has it wrong. It's not about production. It's about how much money you make, what your lifestyle is, and how happy you are.

Definitely; many people just think they need the money when it comes down to it. Happiness is more important.

But think about it, you can't make money unless you close a lot of deals if you're like most loan officers.

Brian, this has been a great interview and I hope our readers take as much from this as possible. Thank you so much for your time and I wish you the best of luck.

Websites You Need To Know About

Every single one of the sites listed below is very informative and needed for you to grow your Mortgage Career. If you want to achieve the level of success that everyone you just read about has, you need to drop everything you're doing and go to these websites right now.

www.MortgageMarketingGenius.com

www.MortgageMarketingMaverick.com

www.ACE-Report.com

www.504Experts.com

www.LoanOfficerSuccess.com

www.ReverseMortgageSuccess.com/ISB

www.MortgageMarketingWhiz.com/ISB

www.WhatBrianUses.com

www.TracyTolleson.com

www.MortgageWebSuccess.com

www.MortgageMarketingMinute.com

www.NARLO.com

www.NARLO.com/free

www.RadioForProfits.com

www.TeleClassRiches.com

www.ThePerfectMortgageSystem.com

www.DanKennedy.com

www.ThePhenomenon.com

www.TomHopkins.com

About the Authors

Nate Kennedy is a very successful Business Owner running multiple companies. He started his thirst for business at the age of eighteen when he attended the Ohio University for college. Nate excelled through college and graduated with a degree in Business Administration with a focus in Finance.

After graduating and leaving Ohio, he moved around trying to find his path. Nate was a scuba diving instructor and restaurant manager before becoming a mortgage broker. During his tenure as a mortgage broker Nate worked for two other companies before starting his own company. After many years of long hours and hard work, he is now providing information to teach people to be successful business owners.

Nate has created multiple successful businesses by using systems that helped him escape the rat race. He has created

Nate Kennedy

streamlined systems that minimize company cost and allow him to work on his businesses instead of in his businesses. His first business adventure and toughest learning experience was starting his own mortgage company. He spent hundreds of thousands of dollars on doing things the wrong way for a business. That money has proven to be a valuable experience as he now starts a new business every year and reaches high gross profits systematically.

Nate now owns and operates four successful businesses that function without him spending fourteen-hour days in the office. He began a journey of making work and life simpler. This journey has come full circle and he is able to spend quality time with his family and travel as he chooses. All this while his businesses function on a proven profit producing system. Nate has created businesses that produce a high incomes, while working less and enjoying life more.

Mark Evans DM is the author of many of the top Real Estate Courses available today. He got his start in Real Estate Investing by doing landlording and rehabbing, like so many people do, and he's literally done it all, at one point or another. So, after 10 years, he's doing what he started out wanting to do...he's giving back.

But, when he first began is Real Estate Investing career, it started out like probably most people—he was scattered and unfocused and unsure of how to achieve his dream. He had no cash and terrible credit, but was determined to seek out a way to make his dream come true with Real Estate Investing.

Also, like most, he wasn't born with a lot and faced many challenges along the way. He came from a very small town where living paycheck to paycheck was the norm...and still is. Though, there's nothing wrong with that if that makes you happy, he knew that he wanted a different life for himself. The life he envisioned was one filled with traveling, spending time with his loved ones, taking time out to enjoy his hobbies, writing, reading success books, creating successful students and masterminding with the top coaches of the world, just to name a few.

Mark Evans DM enjoying his Florida view

So, he dove into educating himself about Real Estate investing, made a lot of mistakes along the way, developed many new strategies that helped him to get it right in half the time, and is now living that exact life he envisioned. His goal is to help others live their ideal life and realize their dreams, complete with Success, Happiness, Financial Freedom, Abundance, Prosperity and Wealth!

CONTACTING THE AUTHORS

Nate Kennedy has a very busy schedule—working on his businesses and spending time growing new resources for the future success of other business owners. He is consistently striving for excellence in business as well as helping his students propel forward to become more profitable, all through using systems.

Nate is always looking for opportunities to help those individuals that understand that success is a lifestyle. Those who are committed to achieving their goals may have a chance to take advantage of Nate's coaching, books, teleseminars, and live seminars. Please contact Nate's office at the web address below to see if you qualify for his available programs.

Nate Kennedy may also be available for speaking and seminar engagements, mentoring, consulting, marketing and/or interviews, both for TV and radio.

To contact Nate Kennedy directly,
go to www.NateKennedy.com

Mark Evans DM has a busy schedule—working his Real Estate Investing business and traveling across the world with his family…all while continuing to strive for excellence in business as well as in helping his students propel forward to become more profitable, all through using systems.

However, he is always looking for opportunities to help those individuals that understand that success is a lifestyle. Those who are committed to achieving their goals may have the chance to take advantage of Mark's coaching, books, teleseminars and live workshops. Please contact Mark's office at the web address below to see if you qualify for his available programs.

Mark Evans DM may also be available for speaking and seminar engagements, mentoring, consulting, marketing and/or interviews, both for TV and radio.

To contact Mark Evans DM directly,
go to www.MarkEvansDM.com